Reflective Assessment

Its Purposes, Methods, and Effects on Learning

Kathleen and James Strickland
Slippery Rock University

Boynton/Cook Publishers
HEINEMANN
Portsmouth, NH

Boynton/Cook Publishers, Inc.
A subsidiary of Reed Elsevier Inc.
361 Hanover Street
Portsmouth, NH 03801-3912

Offices and agents throughout the world

The authors and publisher thank those who generously gave permission to reprint borrowed material:

Figure 3.5 from "Portfolios—The Story Behind the Story" by Sheryl Mondock. From *Language Arts* (Vol. 86, 1, January 1997). Copyright © 1997 by the National Council of Teachers of English. Reprinted with permission.

Figure 7.1 from *Standards for the English Language Arts* by the International Reading Association and the National Council of Teachers of English. Copyright © 1996 by the International Reading Association and the National Council of Teachers of English. Reprinted with permission.

Library of Congress Cataloging-in-Publication Data
Strickland, Kathleen.
    Reflections on assessment : its purposes, methods, and effects on
  learning / Kathleen and James Strickland.
        p.   cm.
    Includes bibliographical references (p. 213) and index.
    ISBN 0-86709-445-1 (alk. paper)
      1. Educational tests and measurements—United States.
  2. Grading and marking (Students)—United States. 3. Portfolios
  in education—United States. 4. Education--Standards—United
  States.
    I. Strickland, James. II. Title.
    LB3051.S88 1998
    371.26'4—dc21   97-50312
                                                 CIP

Editor: Peter R. Stillman
Production: Melissa L. Inglis
Cover design: Joni Doherty
Manufacturing: Louise Richardson

Printed in the United States of America on acid-free paper
02 01 00 99 98 DA 1 2 3 4 5 6 7 8 9

For Ryan Chase, our first grandson,
whose birth interrupted the writing of this book—
quite joyfully

Contents

Preface

The idea to write this book was born of a need to understand. As in so many areas of inquiry in our professional lives, the subject of assessment and evaluation had become one that we had to pursue. In our teaching we had moved to a transactional approach, and we had continued to learn from listening to our students' voices, both oral and written. One thing we heard, which we were painfully aware of but wished would go away, was that our assessment and evaluation practices didn't reflect what we were teaching. Our assessment and evaluation were still dominated by a behaviorist paradigm. Over the years, we both set out to learn about this topic by reading, researching, and networking with colleagues, and most important, by continuing to listen to our students. We found that it might not be easy, but if we wanted to support student progress and performance and improve our teaching, we had no choice.

At this point we don't profess to have the answers; in fact, as in most areas of inquiry, we have more questions than answers. But we have made progress—hence our *Reflections on Assessment*. In this book we attempt to share what we've learned so far. It's not a cookbook—there are no simple recipes for examining individual learning. Instead, we've filled *Reflections on Assessment* with ideas that good teachers from all over the country have shared with us. We consider this book to be a work in progress; we will always have new questions, and we expect new people in our lives will provide fresh ideas. We always tell our students that they need to network with other professionals. Through talking and questioning, sharing and arguing, we can be challenged and can build our ideas on others'. We hope *Reflections on Assessment* will do that.

Good teachers are professionals who share ideas, and we would like to thank the teachers who gave us their time and opened their classrooms to us, especially Pat Bell, Bob Dandoy, Connie Fleeger, and Tina Shorr at Karns City High School in western Pennsylvania, and Dean Smith, Bob Hankes, Danny Taylor, Jon Tarrant, and Nancy Tarrant at Big Spring High School in Newville, Pa. These teachers practice what they preach. We enjoyed spending time in their classrooms watching their students engage in real literacy activities while their teachers worked to support them as learners.

We would also like to thank the teachers who shared their ideas with us through phone calls, e-mail, and personal correspondence: Jane Blystone, North East High School, Pa.; Esther Broughton, Mesa State College, Grand Junction, Colo.; Jim Burke, Burlingame High School, San Francisco, Calif.; Rick Chambers, Ontario College of Teachers, Canada; Bill Clawson, Santa Monica High School, Calif.; Joette Conger, Downer's Grove High School, Ill.; Jane Cowden, Shippensburg University of Pennsylvania; Elizabeth Dore, Radford University, Va.; Ralph Feather, Derry Area High School, Pa.; Carol Jago, Santa Monica High School, Calif.; Barbara King-Shaver, South Brunswick High School, N.J.; Jim Mahoney, Miller Place High School, N.Y.; Kimberly McWherter, Derry Area High School, Pa.; Maureen Neal, Mesa State College, Grand Junction, Colo.; Eileen Oliver, Washington State University; Janine Rider, Mesa State College, Grand Junction, Colo.; Terrie St. Michel, South Mountain High School, Phoenix, Ariz.; Kathy Simmons, Hempfield Area High School, Pa.; Don Strickland, Penfield High School, N.Y.; Terry Wansor, Hempfield Area High School, Pa.; and our colleagues at Slippery Rock University, Neil Cosgrove, Danette DiMarco, and Diana Dreyer.

We would also like to thank the students who shared their writing and ideas with us: Becky Ayres, Heidi Braun, Louise Jessup, Melanie Rahn, and Sarah Smith of Grand River Collegiate Institute, Kitchner, Ontario; Jami Zimmerman, Mesa State College; Carolyn Baker, Katie Butler, Jamie Sue Crouse, Richard Kessler, Matt Kusic, and Elizabeth Spudy of Hempfield Area High School, Pa.; Heather Meloy, Derry Area

High School, Pa.; Karen Patterson, Slippery Rock University, Pa.; and Glenn Wonsettler, Slippery Rock High School, Pa.

We also need to thank Peter Stillman, whose vision shapes the Boynton/Cook imprint, and Melissa Inglis, whose editing abilities continue to produce quality professional publications.

Finally, we would invite readers to use *Reflections on Assessment* as a point to proceed from, knowing that there are no simple answers, but gathering the courage to take the risks needed for real change.

1

Introduction

> Only a deep and ancient prejudice about academic learning keeps us thinking that intellectual competence is achieved by accretion of knowledge and movement through simple logical elements to the complex whole—instead of movement from a crude grasp of the whole to a sophisticated grasp of the whole.
>
> —Grant Wiggins

Not long ago I [Kathleen] agreed to speak at an inservice day on the topic of assessment for about sixty secondary teachers. What could I do for such a short period of time (about two hours) with a group of teachers I didn't know and hadn't worked with before? I decided the only reasonable thing to do would be to try to facilitate a discussion, providing an opportunity for the teachers to share ideas and thoughts.

The teachers divided themselves into small groups in the library and we started with a technique many teachers use when beginning to teach a new topic, making a KWL chart: Know, Wonder, Learn. I asked what they already knew about assessment. They brainstormed everything they could think of when asked to discuss the topic. Although I could sense some hesitation in the groups, the teachers were polite and cooperative for the most part. After sharing responses to what teachers knew about assessment, listing them on an overhead transparency, I then asked them to begin to consider what they wondered about assessment. After ten minutes, the groups shared what they wondered about or what they would like to know, listing questions they had about assessment. We would save the discussion about what we learned about assessment for a later session, after we had had time to find answers to our wonderings.

A gentleman at one of the tables was commenting under his breath to his colleagues (we had spoken briefly as I visited each group while they worked). As he caught my eye, he bravely volunteered to share what I knew many of the teachers were thinking. Politely, but with conviction, he asked, "Why should we change what we've been doing for years? Isn't all this talk about portfolios, performance, and authentic assessment just another fad?" His question was a good one, and it provided the impetus for the rest of that afternoon's discussion.

Teachers are bombarded every year with ideas for change, but the difference between the latest fad and what represents growth depends on our understanding of the learning process. If teachers are satisfied that the methods they are using to assess their students' learning are valid and understandable, then they will see no need for change. Any change mandated by their district would be nothing more than a fad, with which they might try to comply, but which they would quickly discard like many other "fads," neither understanding any need for such a change nor recognizing where the pressure for change came from.

As we continued our discussion that afternoon, it became clear that assessment and evaluation was a topic everyone in that room had questions about. They were concerned with the purpose of assessment, the methods, the political implications, and the consequences. They were concerned with definitions, roles, responsibilities, reactions, and outcomes. They were concerned about the things that impact assessment such as time, class size, training, and parental involvement. What we had discovered at the end of a stimulating two hours was that this was a topic worth pursuing and one that a couple of inservice days couldn't fully address. We decided to begin small, and work together on one method—in this case, portfolios, trying to answer some of the questions we wondered about, while learning together.

As we've discovered more about how we, as teachers, can support the ways people learn, our pedagogies have changed. Workshop approaches, cooperative learning, process orientation, hands-on authentic learning situations are all part of today's classroom because of what we now understand about learning, what research has shown us about supporting learners. We believe if anything about learning is to make sense, our methods of measuring progress and reporting such progress must reflect our pedagogy. Teachers have noticed increasing cases where a score on a multiple-choice test or an SAT score doesn't reflect a particular student's academic life. These teachers are interested in finding ways to measure the depth of their students' thinking, how their students are putting the pieces together, and where to go when their students come to class depending on them for support. Teachers have reached the point where evaluation includes measuring their own as well as their students' success in the classroom.

Teachers have realized that they have to reexamine traditional methods of assessment and evaluation so that they can do what they do best: teach. Consequently, assessment and evaluation are no longer the product of teaching, they are tools that learners and teachers use to support learning.

Jim Burke (1996), an English teacher at Burlingame High School in San Francisco, California, faced a similar situation:

> A few years ago, my department began a dialogue about portfolios and how we determined students' progress. I suggested that we all commit to having students keep writing folders beginning the next September and that we use these as a basis for a practical, ongoing discussion about portfolios—what they were, how they work, why they work. My department chair's reluctance grew into resistance, something which confused me. Eventually she explained that were she to require such a folder in her classes, her students would have next to nothing to put in it. So extreme was her commitment to vocabulary [building] that she devoted nearly 60 percent of her class time to drilling, review-

ing, acting out, writing about words, that they essentially had neither the time nor the cause to write. Others spoke of similar concerns, though [their] reasons varied. What was obvious to me, however, was the extent to which the potential instrument measured not the student so much as the teacher, the department, and, in certain ways, the school itself.

People get passionate about the subject of testing. Some subscribe to it with the zeal of the True Believer, finding in the precision of the AP and SAT an order that keeps the chaos of the world at bay. Others, who often oppose these zealots, wave their own flags, often opposing testing—period—and offering nothing but slings and arrows when testing is discussed. One thing stands out: All seem to know what they believe and they steer by these beliefs with a sailor's calm faith. One must be willing to ask the questions, "What can students do? And what do we need to do to help them do it better?" One must be willing to face the answers these questions [elicit]. Otherwise we end up too often walking around in a fit of passion about what to do. . . .

To assess is to question—constantly, honestly—where you are going and why you are going there. This is particularly difficult and trying when you are a younger teacher or trying something new. People so often want to tell you why you are wrong, how you should do it, how you should test, and how often. Such scrutiny, brought to bear on those who are already questioning their methods, undermines their confidence in their ability and the ideologies that inform their teaching. Teaching, however, allows little time for reflection and so too often we are . . . charging out to do what our instinct told us was right, and sometimes is. So much easier, though, to just give the Scantron test: It's objective, safe, traditional—and often meaningless. Yet it comes with the validation of history: We've always done it this way.

I have taught now for several years. I have tried and failed often—but nobly, and I always try to ask myself the questions necessary to decide how to improve it or whether to toss it. I've had parents call in response to different techniques that involved them—e.g., portfolios—telling me not to ask them to do my job and that they don't need homework since they grad-uated a long time ago. True, these are strange exceptions, never the rule. But when you are new to it all—a feeling which can last a number of years, you can lose your nerve to try certain things that your mentors have led you to believe are right, responsible, and cutting edge. So, too, teachers who have been at it some years find little encouragement for trying to do some-thing new, something different, or something they were led to believe was better. Both the new and experienced teacher try-ing to change find themselves getting cut down . . . they ride into battle armed with confidence in what their teachers have taught them only to find their armor is useless against the worst criticisms one encounters in the field of teaching. If you ques-tion my point, ask yourself why roughly 50 percent of the new teachers leave the field within the first five years; they feel "mangled." If you don't think teachers have tried to test differ-ently and that it has not been emotionally abusive, consider the politics of assessment in the last few years and the toll the oppo-sition to the CLAS test took on its proponents [for a fuller dis-cussion of the CLAS program, see Chapter 7].

These different methods of assessing kids' learning and, as a result, our own teaching, appear to some to be *abnormal* in the excessive, reckless sense . . . [not] the accidental success, the "marvelous act" that grows out of some inspiration you have and foist on your kids before you can think it through. We honor the patient excellence that comes from experience of trying things and learning from them . . . the final measure of our success.

Good, honest assessment necessarily involves risk, call it danger. It demands patience and faith. Often such assessment requires courage: to try, to ask, to fail. Innovative, daring, chal-lenging methods of testing students' learning often invite criti-cism—from parents, other teachers, administrators, and, of course, students. Even we turn against ourselves when some method fails, seeing in it some confirmation of our insecurities instead of an opportunity, a piece of information we can use in the future. Good, honest assessment involves all these elements because whenever we measure others we are also measuring ourselves. (1–4)

Starting Points

Okay, so where do we begin? As Jim says, change is not only difficult but takes time; the most important thing is to start somewhere, take a risk. If we wait for the right time, the moment when a smooth transition will be possible, one bridging the gap between what we've always done and what we'd like to do, the moment will never come. To expect smooth transitions would be somewhat like asking a trapeze artist to look for a smooth transition from one bar to the next. It doesn't exist. At some point one has to let go of the bar and fly. As Howard Kerewsky, Director of Middle Schools in Howard County, Maryland, puts it:

"The bottom line is, you cannot get to trapeze bar B without letting go of trapeze bar A. That is a transformation, not a transition. . . . When you let go of trapeze A, it is going to be hard, whether you do it next week or next year. You have to let go" (Tsujimoto 1991, 14).

Changing the way we assess and evaluate is a transformation; it involves letting go of what is acceptable practice just because it has always been done that way, and moving forward to techniques that inform teaching and learning and support students, even if such techniques are new to the public, administrators, school boards, students, and other teachers. Learning means risk-taking for students and teachers.

The stories of assessment and evaluation told in the following chapters are meant to make the transformation easier by sharing ideas for change. There is no formula, no master design; the ideas shared here are simply starting points for transformation.

Standardized Testing: The Simple Answer to a Complex Issue

Bill Clinton's (1997) State of the Union message focused on education, promising "my number one priority for the next four years is to ensure that all Americans have the best education in the world" (3). His notion of the best education is defined in "three goals," seemingly innocuous: "Every eight-year-old must be able to read; every twelve-year-old must be able to log on to the Internet; every eighteen-year-old must be able to go to college; and every adult American must be able to keep on learning for a lifetime" (3). Regardless of President Clinton's dubious ability to count his goals, we're upset about his notion of how to achieve those goals. The song, "A Call to Action for American Education," is a familiar one—standards and tests:

> First, a national crusade for education standards—not federal government standards, but national standards, representing what all our students must know to succeed in the knowledge economy of the twenty-first century. Every state and school must shape the curriculum to reflect these standards, and train teachers to lift students up to them. To help schools meet the standards and measure their progress, we will lead an effort over the next two years to develop national tests of student achievement in reading and math. . . . By 1999, every state should test every fourth grader in reading and every eighth grader in math to make sure these standards are met. . . . Good tests will show us who needs help, what changes in teaching to make, and which schools need to improve. (4)

And good fences might make good neighbors, teases Robert Frost.

These initiatives have an eerie resemblance to President Bush's American Achievement Tests, announced at the White House on April 18, 1991. The American Achievement Tests were to be "a multidimensional plan which includes a national system of examinations . . . a national report card, funding for model schools, and financial incentives for achievement in what is euphemistically called 'the core academic subjects.' None of the proposals are new," says Elliot Eisner (1992), distinguished professor of education at Stanford University. He says, "Model schools have been present for decades and national testing has been around in one form or another since the National Assessment of Educational Progress emerged almost twenty years ago" (2).

President Clinton will also be testing the teachers: "For years, many of our educators, led by North Carolina's Governor Jim Hunt and the National Board for Professional Teaching Standards, have worked very hard to establish nationally accepted credentials for excellence in teaching. Just five hundred of these teachers have been certified since 1995. My budget will enable one hundred thousand more to seek national certification as master teachers" (4). How will such certification be awarded or evaluated? We certainly hope it will not be through tests such as the National Teacher's Exam (NTE) or Praxis series.

Elliot Eisner (1992) warns of

> the tacit assumption that the most important outcomes of schooling are measurable and that a common test or array of assessment tasks will . . . make meaningful measured comparisons. . . . To describe a human being in numbers alone is to say some important things about that person's features. It is also to neglect those features that do not lend themselves to quantitative description, and the features neglected may be precisely those considered most important for particular purposes. If I want to purchase a pair of shoes for a friend, knowing my friend's shoe size is important, but it is also important to understand what kind of shoes my friend is likely to desire. . . . What is even more troublesome is that almost all of the national proclamations for school reform, including those demanding higher standards and tougher courses, neglect the deeper mission of schooling: The stimulation of curiosity, the cultivation of intellect, the refinement of sensibilities, the growth of imagination, and the desire to use these unique and special human potentialities. (3)

President Clinton (1997) may challenge us by saying "Education is a critical national security issue for our future, and politics must stop at the schoolhouse door," but that over-simplifies the complexity of measuring where we're going and how we can tell if we've gotten there. Yes, the standardized tests are changing, and that in itself is a reflection of the dissatisfaction of teachers who are aware of the limitations of testing, yet an end to standardized testing is nowhere in sight.

As much as we would like to advise teachers to put aside any consideration of standardized tests because these instruments neither help our teaching nor our students' learning, we are also realists. The pressure is so great on high school students to perform well on SAT tests that one novelist, Diane Mott Davidson (1993), makes it the maelstrom for her murder mystery, *The Cereal Murders*. The students, the parents, and the teachers are under such competitive pressure that someone is killing for good grades. Davidson captures the tension: "When he wasn't doing homework, he pored over tomes on test-taking and SAT review. Along with the rest of his class, Julian had taken the PSATs his sophomore year and the SATs his junior year. But this third time was *it*, he told me, the big one, make or break, do or die. These were the scores the colleges looked at to make their decisions" (217). These tests have become so much a part of our culture that Davidson can use them to cook her story.

Unfortunately, tests will still be used for grouping, tracking, funding, politicking, and entrance to colleges and universities. Teachers, however, can put the importance of such testing in perspective: Students who are readers score highest on standardized tests (the use of language in context helps students' vocabulary grow, not the memorized word lists regurgitated on weekly tests), and nothing helps students become better writers the way writing does, not grammar drills, spelling tests, or diagramming sentences. Knowing this, teachers should be confident that when they allow students to read, react, write, and communicate, teachers are doing what they are paid to do—helping their students learn. In the process, not only will their students do as well or better on the tests given, they will receive much more than if they had been in a classroom that prepared them only for a standardized test, an exam that has to do with predicting success, not fostering it.

Evaluation does not have to mean testing. Testing is simply one of these instruments. When teachers use assessment and evaluation, they must vary the instruments employed and the contexts of evaluation. If teachers are interested in growth, they will choose tests that are open-ended instruments demonstrating what students have learned, instead of multiple-choice, one-answer tests displaying what students have memorized. Authentic evaluation is based on information accumulated to indicate growth, gathered with a variety of instruments, many of which are teacher constructed. Teachers in student-centered classrooms use instruments that record how students use knowledge and where they are in the developmental process. Such teachers also use instruments and techniques that are understandable and valued by the students, the ones who ultimately must be able to use the information in order to set goals for further learning.

Eileen Oliver (1996) says that

> grading in my classes has become easier and easier for me over the years as I continue to give students in all my courses the responsibility for assessment in many forms. For their part, my students appreciate this empowerment, though they find it the hardest part of the work they do. . . . When class is finished, there is very little grading for me to do. As a result of several assessments determined all along the way, assessment is quite easy. Students have spent the semester with topics of interest that they have generated by themselves. Their evaluations of several activities have afforded them the opportunity to do some self-assessment and allowed others to evaluate on the basis of standard criteria. When it comes to determining a final grade, students pretty much know what to expect—or at least they should. (2, 7)

Definitions of Learning

Before a teacher or district or department can begin discussing various assessment and evaluation strategies or begin to develop a philosophy of assessment to drive such strategies, it is necessary to be clear about what is being assessed. Before setting criteria, standards, or benchmarks, we have to consider what is meant by "learning." Elsewhere we've written about paradigm shifts and philosophies (Strickland and Strickland 1993; 1996), but we believe teachers often get caught up in the window-dressing of education—curriculum guides neatly delineating the things students must know.

Grant Wiggins (1993) defines learning and its measurement by pointing out that "understanding is not cued knowledge: Performance is never the sum of drills; problems are not exercises; mastery is not achieved by the unthinking application of algorithms. In other words, we cannot be said to understand something unless we can employ our knowledge wisely, fluently, flexibly, and aptly in particular and diverse contexts" (200).

We've all heard from the media that high school students today don't know very much; they don't know who was president during the Civil War, how many days it takes for the earth to orbit the sun, or how many miles it is from New York to Paris. Authors such as E. D. Hirsch, Jr., have written books outlining exactly what "cultured" people and even children should know. If only teaching were that easy. Thinking like this is, of course, the product of a belief system in which learning is defined as the transmittal of a body of knowledge from a text or teacher to a learner. If a teacher's goal is to present facts and help students memorize them, then books such as *Cultural Literacy* and attitudes such as those of E. D. Hirsch, Jr., seem believable and even helpful. But, in today's information age, the number of facts that are known or knowable increases exponentially. What facts should be taught? What culture's history is most important to learn about? What music will affect the future? What literature should be taught in the brief years spent in school? Such decisions are not only impossible, but arbitrary. If we believe that our mission as teachers (if we choose to accept it) is to prepare our students to enter the twenty-first century as thinkers, problem solvers, leaders, and contributing members of a technological society that didn't exist fifty years ago, then simply knowing presidents' names, historical dates, and critics' interpretations of great works is not going to prepare them. If teachers want students to learn to look to history for ways to affect tomorrow's world, to enjoy music as an art form and as entertainment, and to read, not only for the twelve or sixteen years they are in school, but as lifelong readers who look to literature for knowledge, truths, questions, and enjoyment, then learning is something different than the transmission of a body of knowledge. So then, how do we teach? How do we decide on curriculum? How do we measure progress?

Serious Thinkers/Interesting Perspectives

Rick Chambers (1997) looks at his students as serious thinkers and problem solvers. He wanted to challenge his thirty-four senior students to an "investigative, hands-on, practical, and yet reflective approach" to his "literature course, *To Sell One's Soul*, a reasonably depressing, albeit inclusive, collection of readings focusing on compromise, values, morality, life, and death—from Dr. Faustus to King Lear to Graham Greene." Rick relays the experience:

> After the first few weeks of class, it became apparent that these young people were serious thinkers who had some interesting perspectives on life and morality, and that an action research assignment [what Macrorie (1988) and others call an I-search paper] might play well into their general knowledge and interests, while expanding their reading and critical thinking. Previously, independent study projects had been exclusively literature focused—a student was invited to select three novels (or equivalent—plays, collections of poetry, or short stories) on a

theme or by one author, find some literary criticism, present an oral presentation to the class on the theme or author, and then write a critical essay on a topic that grew out of the oral presentation. My experience with this kind of project increasingly demonstrated that the students never really knew what to read or explore in their independent studies, because the whole idea of a theme or even a canonically correct or appropriate author was reasonably foreign, if not simply dull to them. So, action research would be different.

After brainstorming some ideas, and covering the blackboard with various tangents related to the ideas, I introduced the idea of the action research projects. The process was simple, from my perspective: Each student had to:

- identify a research interest,
- state why he/she was interested in that topic,
- figure out what kind of evidence could be gathered,
- decide how to share the information with the class,
- write about the learning that had occurred, and
- reflect on the entire project in writing.

I wanted the students to demonstrate some integrated learning skills, and to practice what we had been preaching about—applying knowledge from one area to help with understanding in another. Therefore, when the fashion design student said she wanted to investigate the morality of the North American obsession with beauty, I was interested. She was going to read *A Portrait of Dorian Gray*, several nonfiction titles on the business of beauty, and use some of the information that she had acquired in her sociology course. She was also going to talk to people in her modeling course and to plastic surgeons in the city. Another student wanted to pursue the Holocaust in more detail. She had read *The Diary of Anne Frank* and was working on *Schindler's List*, but she really wanted to read the book of a Holocaust survivor who lived in her apartment building. She rode the elevator with this woman frequently and had only recently discovered that she had written her memoirs. So, this student read the books, but also conducted a fascinating interview with the survivor, which became the centerpiece of the student's oral presentation to the class.

Interestingly, students often applied what they had learned in history, science, sociology, and other classes to their pursuit of these topics in English. The students' previous experience with the topic, tied to their new reading and investigation, broadened their knowledge and fanned their interest. As well, the nature of action research lent itself to the inclusion of contemporary news stories, recently released films, and popular fiction. The assessment for the project was organized as it had been for the independent study projects: process (demonstrated by a work folder which would contain all of the rough notes, journal entries, reflections, topic sheets, interview notes, and anything else that seemed germane to the project), oral presentation, and written presentation.

Students' reflections on the action research were particularly revealing, because they demonstrated the involvement and engagement that students had with their topics, and the process of their learning. For example, one student . . . whose topic was alcoholism—inspired by a personal family experience—talked about the complexity of something that she thought was going to be straightforward: "When I first began my research I was planning on talking about alcoholism in general. However, this was much more difficult than I had thought. Little did I know that there was no alcoholism *in general*; it proved to be a much more complex topic than I had thought. After I had read my first book, I thought I was off to a pretty good start. However, when I finished reading the [second], I realized that the two books contradicted each other. I began to panic slightly, but as I continued my research I began to realize that the contradictions actually formed a pattern. I came to the realization that there were basically two main theories pertaining to the cause of alcoholism; it was then that I changed my game plan. I decided to focus on the debate about whether alcoholism is a disease or whether it is a result of poor moral choices."

What I've been trying to convince students of for years is that school is just a way to develop their critical thinking abilities: the study of English is a means to an end, and not an end in itself. Using their critical thinking, analyzing, reading, writing, speaking, interviewing, presenting, and synthesizing skills, students in this action research project were able to focus on topics that were interesting to them, and as a result of their problem-solving abilities and presentation skills, became interesting for the rest of us too. (1–2)

Rick defined for himself and with students what learning is. With this understood, Rick and his students were ready to assess the process and the product to continue learning. How do we help students use assessment as a tool to set goals and evaluate what they have learned?

Learning as Meaning-Making

Teachers must come to regard learning as a process of meaning-making—not an accumulation of skills, but a process of actively constructing meaning. We read a newspaper article criticizing first-year college students for not knowing that the phrase, "of the people, by the people, for the people," was from the Gettysburg address. We couldn't help wondering why the author wasn't concerned about the *messages* contained in such famous historical speeches and how such messages apply to our world in the 1990s. In school, we've given students the impression that they are to learn things, instead of learning how to learn. If we believe that learning is a lifelong activity, then formal schooling must be about that process. The rest is incidental. Writing, for example, cannot be evaluated as though it were simply grammar exercises, spelling, five-paragraph essays, and assigned research papers on teacher-generated topics (although such evaluations are relatively easy to quantify).

In many classrooms across the country, students are reading for real purposes and using their interpretations of what they read to think, to question, to research, and to write, much the way Rick's students did when they investigated the obsession with beauty and cause of alcoholism. When language learning is viewed this way, assessment and evaluation must go far beyond weekly tests on the parts of language. Writing and reading must be regarded as meaning-making processes, ways to think and communicate thoughts, ideas, and feelings. If students are to grow as readers and writers, assessment and evaluation—which have language growth as their purpose—must include students' reading and writing behaviors as well as their written products. The same is true in other academic areas such as science and mathematics.

During the State of the Union address, President Clinton (1997) and Secretary of Education Richard Riley (a lawyer and former governor) lauded the efforts of eighth-grade students from northern Illinois who competed in the Third International Math and Science Study, "a test that reflects the world-class standards our children must meet for the new era. And those students in Illinois tied for first in the world in science and came in second in math." Although these students and their efforts should be recognized, what Elliot Eisner finds

> particularly perplexing [about reports such as these] is the substitution of slogans for reflective thought. Consider our need to be number one. The image of America being first in mathematics and science seems initially attractive. We all like to be first. But upon reflection just what does being first in mathematics and science mean? Is it assumed that being first in an international race means that we not only have a national curriculum, but a *world* curriculum to be first in? Does it mean that our students come out first on a *world* examination? Is it assumed that being first in mathematics and science will insure a better life and good jobs? Clark Kerr's (1991) analysis of the feckless relationship between the quality of schooling and our nation's economic condition undercuts any argument that there is a strong causal relationship between test scores and the state of our economy. As far as I can tell, there has been no rationale, compelling or otherwise, to support the aspiration to be first, aside from the almost knee-jerk reaction that first is a good thing to be. (1992, 3)

Mathematicians know that what is important is thinking mathematically, solving problems, and making sense of the world of mathematics. Tests are not the only way to evaluate a student's mathematical sense. In sciences, facts and formulas are only tools to a much higher order of learning that science teachers assess through observation, writing to learn, and demonstration. Discovery and scientific process are the backbone of scientific thinking.

Meeting Student Needs

Students learn by constructing meaning from the world around them. Curriculum in a transactional classroom is not a prescribed course of study; instead it is learning that occurs when students are engaged in making meaning, learning what is worthwhile, useful, and easiest to learn, as Frank Smith (1988) tells us in *Joining the Literacy Club*. Teachers need to organize curriculum by student needs rather than a prescribed curriculum or set program. Some teachers have difficulty letting student needs drive instruction, especially high school teachers who are handed a prescribed curriculum and told that the content must be "covered." We titled our earlier book, *UN-Covering the Curriculumm*, because we believe good teachers provide experiences that allow students opportunities to demonstrate what decisions they, as language users, are interested in and capable of making, opportunities to develop certain insights and an improved level of content knowledge. Jeff Golub (1993) remarks that "the pressure to 'cover the curriculum' is perhaps the most direct and immediate pressure that teachers feel. Too often, the curriculum becomes divorced from the teachers who teach it. . . . When one must *cover* items—and usually there are far too many items in the curriculum anyway to be covered adequately—one tends to focus on teaching content instead of teaching students" (3).

The temptation is to let predetermined curriculum drive teaching, hoping that students will score highly on school-constructed or state-administered exams. Many teachers, however, resist the temptation and develop ways to meet student needs and interests while still *covering* the curriculum. Such teachers base their teaching on the belief that learning must be authentic and purposeful. A colleague of Rick Chambers (1993) at the Grand River Collegiate Institute had just finished covering *The Great Gatsby* with a senior English class, having covered the material in a very traditional, socratic, chapter-by-chapter method. The teacher decided to take a risk and teach the next novel, *The Stone Angel*, by Canadian author Margaret Laurence, in a more student-centered fashion, asking the students to record periodically in their journals their thoughts about events, characters, style, settings, moods, or anything else that occurred to them in the course of reading the novel. Class and group discussions were also held concerning ideas that arose from the novel. Completed journals were eventually submitted to the teacher, and the students highlighted the four or five entries that they were particularly interested in having their teacher read for evaluation.

Given a choice of novels to write about on their examination, more than 90 percent of the students chose to write about *The Stone Angel*, responding to the traditional essay question with authority, carefully developed organization, and a mature understanding and appreciation of the novel. This teacher not only covered the material but found that, instead of simply telling students teacher-known information, the student-centered approach let students learn the material, expressing insights that they saw perhaps for the first time and sharing it with others by writing it down.

Assessment and Evaluation: Co-dependent but Different

For a long time the terms *assessment* and *evaluation* were used synonymously and interchangeably with terms such as *grading* and *reporting*, each referring to the mysterious scores imposed on learners, quantitatively determined by their teachers or by testing companies. Most important, these scores were terminal, signaling the end product of a course, a unit, or a school career. Actually, each of these terms—assessment, evaluation, grading, reporting—means something quite different.

Assessment refers to a collection of data, information that enlightens the teacher and the learner, information that drives instruction. Good teachers assess constantly, performing the first stage of a recursive process. They observe what is happening in their classrooms—"kid-watching" as Yetta Goodman (1978) would say—and then talk to students and ask them questions about their learning (conferencing as writing teachers do or interviewing their subjects as naturalistic researchers do). They devise ways to record their observations. Good teachers assess and adjust their teaching based on their assessments. They also share assessments with their students, so students can adjust their performances to meet criteria for personal expectations or those imposed on them by their teachers or by others.

Assessment is something that teachers have done informally and almost routinely. They are assessing when they say at the end of class, "that went well today" or "Whew, they just don't seem to get this. What should I do next to clear this up?" In the same way that good teachers assess their own performance, they constantly look for indications of student understanding or progress, either as individuals or as a group. Although this type of assessment takes many forms and is managed in a variety of ways (as discussed in later chapters), two features are important: Assessment is ongoing and is a collection of information—*data*, facts that help teachers put the pieces together, much like how Rick's students collected data when looking for answers to their problems. Today teachers are recognized by the profession as researchers in their classrooms, gathering and analyzing evidence of learning, and using such evidence to help all concerned—students, parents, administrators, and themselves as teachers—understand the learning processes of individuals and groups of learners. Teachers investigate learning, gathering evidence to illustrate not only that their students are learning, but what it is that they are learning.

Evaluation, although sometimes used in the same ways as the term assessment, is the next step in a recursive process. Evaluation is the product of assessment, a step further toward understanding and drawing conclusions. After gathering data—information and evidence—teachers, like researchers, must put the pieces together, evaluating the products of their efforts and the progress of their students. This evaluation is neither subjective—an opinion based on what the teacher instinctively feels—nor simply an average of scores. Rather, evaluation uses a variety of assessment techniques and validates its conclusions by investigating relationships in the data, triangulating the data, analyzing what is gathered from a multiplicity of perspectives. Evaluation in this sense is helpful to learners rather than simply judgmental, understandable rather than mysterious, and anticipated by learners when they have been informed and involved in the assessment process.

"Our evaluation practices operationally define what really matters for students and teachers," says Elliot Eisner (1992), critic of the standardized testing industry. "If our evaluation practices do not reflect our most cherished values, they will undermine the values we cherish. We need, in other words, to approach educational evaluation not simply as a way of scoring students, but as a way in which to find out how well we and our students are doing in order to do better what we do. Evaluation should be regarded as an educational medium, an important source for school improvement. And what it addresses should reflect the educational values we believe important" (5).

Reporting is the third step of this recursive process. After assessing and evaluating, teachers have the responsibility of sharing their evaluations with the interested parties, primarily the students but also their parents, administrators, other teachers, and of course, the general public. Reporting is valuable to those outside the classroom who have not been involved in the assessment and evaluation process. Traditionally such reporting has been limited to report card grades and standardized test scores.

Grading is the assignment of a numerical score, letter, or percentage to a product. Terry Wansor (1996), former chair of the Hempfield Area English department, makes it clear to his students that "assessment and grading are not the same things." Terry allows his students to choose the works they wish to be graded for the marking period and uses a grading rubric that is adapted from sources such as the Pennsylvania Writing Assessment Holistic Scoring Guide (see Figure 3.6) and a rubric from William Irmscher's (1984) *Teaching Expository Writing*. "In all my courses, my assessment of writing occurs *during the composing process* by my providing written (and sometimes spoken) commentary on several of the drafts; my responses along with peer comments usually give the students as much [feedback] as they seem to want. . . . [However,] when I grade a paper, that's all the kid gets—a grade, no comments, no suggestions, no coaching, no strokes, no encouragement, just a grade"—because the paper is no longer in process, and suggestions are not useful at this point. Terry expresses an uneasiness about the value of grading. It is still something foreign to his sense of learning. He says, "I never have students grade themselves or each other, though they often evaluate and assess each other's and their own work. Grading, when it is done—once per quarter, in addition to a midterm and final exam—is done solely by me, and what I do is mostly add numbers to calculate a percent average. This more or less meaningful symbol is then passed along to the rest of the universe as a token of progress made by the given student."

Traditionally grades for the report card have been the standard way to report to learners how well they have met the expectations for an assignment or course. However teachers are not obliged to follow the norm. For example, Eileen Oliver (1996) says her

> students do the reading (or they don't), write critiques which cause
> them to interact effectively with the text (or not), and present

and/or respond to interesting, thoughtful questions, comments, or criticisms during discussions. I typically comment and give papers a plus (+), a check (✓), or a minus (–). At first students are annoyed with this procedure, especially the ones who have done a good job. They want more pay for their efforts. They soon realize, however, that my expectations for the class are quite high. I am prepared to give everyone a plus—though it doesn't always turn out that way. They also learn that anything lower is not very good. Mostly, everyone gets the maximum credit several times. . . . Students (and I) can look over these responses and give a pretty accurate account of the students' "earnings" for this part of the course. Without having to put a letter grade on every piece of paper they turn in, we have an assessment of written critiques. (3)

In later chapters, we will describe systems of reporting that reveal much more about the learner and what has been learned, through portfolios, narratives, public celebrations, and summative checklists of criteria.

Supporting Student Growth

Obviously, teachers need to evaluate student performance, and many teachers are convinced that more honest, worthwhile, and humane ways exist to assess than have been employed in traditional classrooms. Our rationale for assessment and evaluation must be based on philosophical principles of teaching and learning (Harp 1994). Assessment and evaluation must grow out of a belief in student and teacher empowerment. Effective assessment and evaluation must be based on teaching within a transactional philosophy of learning and must have student support and growth as its goals. Many school districts and even state departments of education try to impose an evaluation system on teachers, one that they may even call "holistic"; however, unless the teachers understand and accept the philosophical underpinnings out of which such "holistic" evaluation systems grow, imposed systems cannot work.

Support Authentic Learning

Most would agree that assessment and evaluation should be developmentally appropriate and culturally sensitive. Unfortunately, many of the instruments that are commonly used in education are biased in regard to gender, ethnicity, and socioeconomic factors. Students come to school as proficient language users; however, their language may not always be the language of the academy or the language of privilege. Standards have a place, but that place should not make students feel excluded from the ranks of the academic elite, those who have set the "standards" in the first place.

Many standardized tests have been determined to be culturally biased, yet they are still given and used to control students' destinies. For example, the residents of western Pennsylvania, where we now live, have a "to be" deletion rule for certain grammatical constructions, a rule that they are unaware of for the most part. A native western Pennsylvanian would say (and write, unless made aware of the distinction through hyper-literate schooling), "My car needs washed," instead of "My car needs to be washed." We have traced the origins of this construction to a rule derived from the Scots who settled the area, a construction considered quite proper in formal Scottish grammar. An assessment instrument such as a "spot the error in the sentence" grammar test might have any number of sentences using "to be" constructions that conflict with regional usage. How many other variations must be accounted for if standardized tests were to begin to consider regional dialects, racial/ethnic dialects, class dialects, and gender differences?

Students in secondary and postsecondary classrooms must be afforded opportunities to make choices about their language and about their learning. Teachers in today's classrooms must realize that their task is not to make all students speak or write or think according to artificial preordained standards; their task is to help students develop as learners, affording them opportunities to make choices about matters such as dialect or lan-

23

guage, choices that develop as students perceive the need for them. Therefore, it is up to classroom teachers to use assessment and evaluation techniques that value who students are and what they bring to the learning situation.

Being developmentally and culturally appropriate means looking at assessment and evaluation from the learner's viewpoint. Terrie St. Michel (1993) of South Mountain High School in Phoenix, Arizona, says that her first three years of teaching English in an inner-city high school were spent trying to do everything according to the policies and procedures set by the school and district. Her approach to teaching was strictly traditional. But Terrie confesses that she began to discover that her students had opinions, desires, questions, and abilities that they wanted to explore, but they did not know how. She started by recognizing who her urban students were: "kinesthetically oriented students who interacted with each other and their environment physically" and who perceived reading, writing, and classroom discussions as "passive activities" (11).

Terrie says that she "started asking questions and looking for activities which would engage my students in the learning process in such a way that the students would become a part of what they were learning rather than disassociated bystanders simply going through the motions." She says that she worked to "project a sensitive awareness" of how her students perceived learning, that she "understood how they felt and would not judge them according to my perceptions." She introduced a unit called *Developing a Sense of Self* because her students were "at a point in their lives where they are discovering the 'who,' 'what' and 'how' they are." Terrie believes that better understanding has "encouraged [her] students to become active participants in the learning process—helping to formulate test questions, grading each other's papers with concern for helping rather than humiliating, investing more honestly in discussions and sharing their own feelings, relating their experiences to the content, forming a community of learners who work together and notice each other, taking responsibility for their own choices, and more readily accepting challenges. In short, their learning experience is more personally fulfilling because they are investing more of their person in the learning process." Terrie then builds on their development of self when teaching traditional course content, such as Shakespeare's *Macbeth*. Her students found that they could relate to Macbeth's woes. They connected Macbeth's reliance on the witches' predictions and his reluctance to defy Lady Macbeth to their experiences of peer pressure from gangs—from killings of rival gang leaders to misinterpreting gang signs to betrayal of gang loyalty. Terrie says, "These discussions precede writing assignments in which the students present their perceptions and explain their observations" (11). Terrie aligned the requirements imposed by the school and district with the needs of her students using techniques that afforded her students the opportunity to grow in directions they felt were important for their lives.

Teachers should focus on students' strengths rather than on deficiencies. For years, educators have let students know what was wrong with them. Their papers have been "red-penned" and the number wrong marked at the top, and what little written comment appeared always conveyed a message about how to "fix" what was wrong with their work. In life, people learn and grow based on what they know, what they are good at, and what their strengths are. Teachers must be sensitive to this distinction; they must genuinely believe in all students' abilities and strive to help students see the possibilities of future learning.

If teachers believe in their students' right to be all that they are capable of being, then teachers have a responsibility to communicate this belief to their students. They must communicate a respect and interest in what students are able to accomplish. They must help students recognize what they can do, and help them set attainable goals for themselves. Then, teachers support students as each works toward these goals. Perhaps this is what the topic of assessment and evaluation is all about. Assessment and evaluation must primarily be for the students themselves, so they might recognize their own strengths and move forward to meet goals they have set for themselves.

Thoughts for Further Inquiry

1. Using a KWL chart, list all that you (or your group) know about assessment and evaluation. Next, list all that you wonder about. Use this list to guide your reading and discussion throughout this book.
2. Think of your experiences as a learner and/or as a teacher. How did assessment and evaluation influence you as a learner? as a teacher?
3. What is your definition of learning? Based on that definition, what are the goals you have set for yourself as a learner? What are the goals you have set for your teaching? How does your curriculum support these goals?
4. Discuss differences between assessment, evaluation, grading, and reporting. Why do you think these terms are used so interchangeably? As a learner, which of these is most important to you? Why? As a teacher, which is most important? Why?
5. Interview teachers and ask them to define and discuss assessment, evaluation, grading, and reporting. What did you learn from these interviews?

2

Assessment Drives Instruction

The central function of assessment, therefore, is not to prove whether or not teaching or learning have taken place, but to improve the quality of teaching and learning, and to increase the likelihood that all members of society will acquire a full and critical literacy.

— NCTE/IRA Standards for the Assessment
of Reading and Writing

An interactive curriculum depends on a teacher knowing how his or her students are reacting to instruction, what lines of inquiry they wish to pursue, what research they need to conduct, and what tools they need to move forward with their learning. Such a curriculum, one blending student interests and needs with the required curriculum, depends on continuous assessment. Ongoing assessment does much more than inform evaluation; one of assessment's functions is to drive instruction.

Teachers use assessment to help them reflect on their own teaching. "When I think of assessment, evaluation, and instruction, my attention immediately focuses on my students," says Terrie St. Michel (1997) of South Mountain High School in Phoenix. "I ask myself, 'Where are they in terms of their learning? . . . What do I hope they will learn? . . . How does [my course] relate to my students' lives now and in the future?' . . . You must know where you are and where you want to go if you are to maximize the steps for getting there, [and] assessment provides an important first step." From the first week of class, Terrie begins assessing her students' abilities and says that this becomes "the driving force behind my instruction." She even uses these early assignments for a self-evaluation assignment in which she asks the students to read their earlier writings and "write a reaction/reflection essay describing their growth—from a personal perspective and in terms of their writing skills" (1).

Unfortunately, teachers don't always draw the best conclusions from their assessments. Take the case of a writing teacher who noticed "a pervasive spread of grade inflation" that she believed was the result of an overdependence on process writing and peer editing: "support from teacher and peers at every stage of the process—brainstorming, drafting, revising, and editing." She decided that "the best way to control grade inflation is to nip budding over-dependency." She used her assessment to drive her instruction.

> I do not read every draft or entire portfolios, and on those drafts to which I do respond I try to resist the temptation to over-explain marginal comments, especially on mechanics. I simply circle usage or mechanical errors the first time they surface, not every subsequent time they reappear, and the student finds the explanation in their *Handbook*, seeking an explanation from me only if stumped. . . . I no longer routinely build individual writing conferences into the syllabus for every paper . . . For years I spoon-fed process writing to my students and baby-sat them through my courses. As a mother of four, how could I have forgotten that the more you do for learners of any age, the more they expect of you? Now I expect maturity and independence from the classes, and they take this challenge as a compliment. (O'Donnell 1994, 8)

Others can make the same assessments looking at similar incidents in the classroom and come to different conclusions: Someone else might see assessment and evaluation serving quite different models of learning. Diana Dreyer (1994) sees this as "a collision of models [of teaching] . . . in the case in question, teaching the entire writing process, [which results] in products predicated on student choice, collaboration, revision, editing, etc.—and then holding up the traditional, product-based pedagogy as a template for [grading] assessment" (9). Diana believes that

> without congruent [models of assessment and] evaluation, we wind up with grades as mysterious in nature to students as the process of how writers write is to inexperienced writers who've never had the benefit of exposure to the variety of workable strategies that writers employ. Worse still, we're once again setting up our students for failure, sending out a very mixed message: learn to use these strategies and see how you grow as a writer; then I as your teacher will pull the rug out from under you, doing the time-honored error count thing—never mind the meaning you managed to convey. (10)

Thus, it is clear that assessment and evaluation must be working to serve the same ends.

Traditionally, what we teach is detailed and outlined before the school year even begins. We're still driven by the "scope and sequence charts," the course of study prescribed by the state, the district, and the publishing company. The course of study, the textbook, and often even the exams are predetermined, so for some it doesn't matter what the students already know, or what they are interested in, or what is happening in the world that might have an impact on their course of study. A good teacher can be counted on to *cover* the curriculum. But as Elliot Eisner (1992) reminds us,

> If teaching is weak or insensitive, whatever virtues the curriculum might possess will be for naught. The teacher is the prime mediator of life in the classroom and the quality of teaching ought to be a primary concern of school improvement. . . . Our evaluation practices operationally define what really matters for students and teachers. If our evaluation practices do not reflect our most cherished values, they will undermine the values we

cherish. We need, in other words, to approach educational evaluation not simply as a way of scoring students, but as a way in which to find out how well we and our students are doing in order to do better what we do. (5)

As teachers we're accountable for more than covering the curriculum. Of course, we are all concerned about knowledge and about skills, but teaching takes place *during* the process. A good teacher supports students as they *construct* knowledge together and use the skills necessary to the process. By the time a product has been produced for evaluation, there are no longer any teaching opportunities. Thus, assessment during the process must provide those opportunities and drive instruction. In a transactional classroom, learning results from inquiry. Because knowledge isn't separate from life and culture, and because learning is individual, complex, and recursive, neither predictable by age or gender, nor linear and sequential, it's necessary for teachers to use techniques that organize and manage what is happening with individual students in secondary classrooms. With 100–150 students, teachers need ways to structure and manage the daily activities of each course while supporting the individual growth of each of these students. Knowing students as individuals means being able to talk with an individual student or parent or administrator about that student's progress and growth and use specifics, not just vague numbers or percentages. What are the student's strengths? How are they best exhibited? What are their needs? their goals? How will they work toward these goals? Questions such as these aren't answered by a grade. They are outgrowths of the process of learning—a process that is organic, unique to the individuals involved, and collaborative between teacher and students. However, to find answers, teachers need to know how to gather the data and how to analyze the information, much the way anthropological and sociological researchers do. Such gathering and analysis requires a knowledge of qualitative assessment techniques, such as keeping anecdotal records, conducting interviews, compiling checklists, and carrying on dialogue discussions.

Assessment by Observation

Anthropologists and sociologists have long recognized the power of observation as a research tool. In order to learn about a culture, one needs to observe how the culture operates, either as a participant or as an outside observer. Educators are beginning to sense the power of observation in understanding the culture of a classroom and the learning processes of individuals. Like anthropologists and sociologists, teachers are learning to record long, detailed accounts, thick with description so they can later recall specifics and put pieces together to draw conclusions about their classroom culture.

Yetta Goodman (1978) encourages teachers to use the power of observation to learn about their students, engaging in "kid-watching," a term we've mentioned earlier. Kid-watching is possible only in interactive classrooms where students work cooperatively and independently and where the teacher assumes a variety of roles including that of observer. It may be immediately apparent that such a technique can be used only in classrooms where teachers are not always behind lecterns in the front of the room dispensing knowledge. Philosophically, if teachers believe that supporting learners means being able to recognize the behaviors associated with such learning, then teachers must observe their students participating in genuine learning activities. As teachers observe their students using language, science, math, or history, they are able to assess what is happening, recording their observations in a variety of ways. If teachers believe in supporting learners, then assessment by observation occurs continuously.

Teachers who use assessment and evaluation on a daily basis are always searching for patterns, supporting students as they take risks and move forward, and watching in order to better facilitate further learning. They listen to students, talk with students, and try to understand how each student is progressing. If assessment and evaluation are to drive instruction, then they must be a part of the daily life of a classroom, determining what will be taught the next day, the next week, and the next semester. Observation can take many forms, from watching students work together in groups to using checklists during workshop times to watching kids interact in the moments before the bell rings. Observations about student progress can be recorded or documented using a variety of techniques such as anecdotal records, interviews or conferencing, and checklists.

Anecdotal Records

Anecdotal records are meant to be quick notes of observations, items that teachers think they are going to remember but, unless written down, are often forgotten. Anecdotal records may be written for a variety of assessment activities: recording observations of students as they work in class, recording student comments about process or product, recording student responses to situations or tasks, recording how students synthesize what they are learning, and recording questions that they as teachers might have about what they are seeing. They need not be as laborious a task as case study research. When teachers look over their notes, they are able to put pieces together and draw conclusions that would have been more difficult if the observations were not recorded.

For instance, the following entries are typical of a teacher jotting down notes about what she is observing in her class:

9/11—Loretta is bored and wants textbooks; Tanya has the same problem. Maybe I can work out of the old science texts when we talk about the senses. Tanya's becoming vocal about her displeasure. I'll have to try to "wean" them away from these gradually.

9/16—Tim is so improved. What wonders a year of maturation can make. He really seems to be enjoying independent reading. He's only reading about sports heroes, but at least he's reading! It doesn't seem to be just to please adults either. I think I'll try the dialogue journal with him. It may make him feel special, and he needs that attention right now.

9/17—David is a puzzle—very angry! Directing that anger to other kids—acting superior and condescending. He is reading more though. I'm not sure how he feels about what he reads, just as I'm not sure what he feels about anything.

10/9—Robb wrote a fairly decent story today–see lesson notes–I was pleased and so was he! Finally, a bright spot!

10/16—Shannon *still* has great difficulty putting ideas down. There's some improvement but I have to work on her prewriting strategies. Maybe if I get her to talk more before writing it will help. (Strickland 1995, 28)

These short and quickly written entries help the teacher begin to see threads throughout her observations. The anecdotes reveal that Ann Hunter, the teacher, has learned to let her students' needs drive her instruction. Ann says that anecdotal records help her to sort things out; they are a type of writing for discovery. Her musings about her students are much the same as those that cross the minds of every good teacher throughout a day, except that they are written. The reporting, questioning, and projecting show Ann trying to figure out what her students know and how she can help them move forward in their learning. Ann used observation to help her evaluate and support Gary, a student who had met with failure for years in schools and was practically a nonreader:

"Gary is *really* preying on my mind. He's having so much trouble with language, but I'm not sure if it's neurologically based or due to years of failure and frustration. I think I'll try having him talk into a tape recorder for some of his writing. That may not be much better though, because he rambles so much. He decodes on about a third grade level I'd guess, but I don't think he has more than surface comprehension. His handwriting is illegible, and he is unhappy with it—I'll have him try word processing" (Strickland 1995, 29).

Words like "try" and "maybe" indicate that she is a risk-taker, working with her students, talking to them, and discovering their strengths and weaknesses. She does not blame students for what they do not know; she tries to identify strategies that might support them as learners. She does not try to make them fit into a preordained curriculum; instead, she assumes responsibility for finding a way to meet their needs and support them in a timely fashion.

Keeping anecdotal records requires organization and management. Some teachers, like Ann, keep a notebook or log, writing in it at different times of the day. Others use Post-it notes or index cards. Some have a three-ring binder with a tab for each student. Some keep electronic notes, entering notes into a computer file the way nurses in some hospitals now record their notes directly into a patient's file. Other teachers jot down quick observations during the day on a sheet of peel-off blank address labels carried on a clipboard, notes that can be removed at the end of the day and stored in a notebook divided according to classes, a page for each student. This is a particularly efficient method, especially for teachers who are responsible for large numbers of students, as many secondary teachers are. As we all know, some students get noticed naturally—the students who are bright and articulate, the leaders of discussions, and the students who are having academic or personal difficulties. Not only will this system help a teacher identify the needs and strengths of those students, it will also help that teacher identify those students who are between either extreme, the students who haven't been noticed lately, the ones who fall through the cracks. Teachers who use peel-off labels for anecdotal records can look quickly through their notebooks to see which of their students haven't been observed lately. When this happens, the teacher thinks, "What about Tracy? I've recorded nothing for the last two weeks. I'll have to pay closer attention, maybe sit in on a group she's working with or talk with her before class begins."

No matter how teachers decide to manage it, anecdotal records help teachers to become reflective decision makers and make later evaluation more concrete because specific incidents are recorded for reflection and analysis. Using assessments such as these, student needs and interests drive instruction. When teachers know their students better, teachers can tailor instruction and group students together for a variety of instructional purposes.

Interviews/Conferencing

Interviews, another type of qualitative assessment, can take many forms. Jim uses an interview technique early in the semester when he hands an index card to each student to fill out. He asks questions such as, What career or major are you thinking of pursuing? What do you like to do outside of class (hobbies, clubs, sports, interests)? What is the last movie you went to see? Do you own a computer? Do you know how to word process? What is the name of the last book you have read? Do you consider yourself a writer? Students' answers to these questions help Jim to glean information about his students so that he begins to know them as people. We should never discount the importance of knowing our students better. As one student speaker told the audience at our nephew's recent graduation, the teachers who affected him the most were the ones who took the time to know him as a person.

Our students' interests and literacy backgrounds shape their attitudes toward reading and writing. For example, Jim used the information he received from the index cards to alter his instruction to include reading and writing about a self-selected novel as part of his first-year composition class. One young man, who wrote on his index card that he didn't read, couldn't find a novel that he could "get into," although Jim brought a variety of selections to class. Although he started a number of books, Burt would give up after several pages. One Monday morning, Burt came to class and announced that he had found a book, one of the *Fear Street* series by R. L. Stine. Burt was so excited about having a book to read that he wanted his teacher to read it when he was finished. Jim prayed that no one in the class would make some thoughtless comment about the book's reading level or the juvenile following the author had. Luckily, no one did and Burt was able to successfully finish a book, write about it thoughtfully, and see himself as a reader.

At midterm evaluation, one of our colleagues, Diana Dreyer, uses a set of reflective interview questions to help students think about their writing and to emphasize or review the processes they use to write (see Figure 2.1). These interview questions require students to consider audience, purpose, invention, and revision, and become aware of themselves as writers. The interview questions provide one piece of assessment data—collected but ungraded. The reflective nature of the interview prepares the students for an essay Diana will later ask them to write for their final portfolio, one giving specific rationale for the writings in their portfolios. Interviews like these help teachers to see their classrooms as populated by individuals as well as seeing it as a whole.

Figure 2.1   Midterm Reflective Questionnaire

Please attach your answers to this questionnaire to the top of your drafts, followed by your latest draft with all previous drafts and prewrites in reverse chronological order below.

1. Who's your audience for this paper? (no somebodies, anybodies, people who are interested in family, etc.; be precise)
2. What is the paper's purpose, the effect you want to have on the audience?
3. In what ways did you gather ideas for this paper?
4. What changes did you make between the first and final draft—and why did you make these changes?
5. What was the hardest thing for you to do as you drafted and revised this paper?
6. What aspect of this paper are you happiest about?
7. What did you learn from writing this paper—about your writing process and/or your topic?

Another type of interview takes place when teachers conference; that is, they speak to their students one-on-one about their writings. Conferencing helps students in workshop class-rooms discover what to do next with their learning, and teachers find that conferencing allows them to assess the progress and needs of students as individuals and the class as a whole. During conferences, students get an opportunity to share self-assessments and teachers take note of areas that might need to be addressed in a minilesson during direct teaching to a group or the entire class. Such assessments help drive instruction.

Jane Blystone (1997a), a teacher at North East High School in North East, Pennsylvania, says she got the idea that assessments help drive instruction "from an old black and white film I saw about the way Ray Bradbury writes his stories. Bradbury spends a great deal of time asking his peers to react to his work and relies heavily on their understanding of his writing as a key to his revision." Jane decided to have her students act as Bradbury readers for each other.

> When we begin the short story unit, we spend about four peri-ods working on character development. We try to learn what the character looks like, how the character acts and reacts in a variety of situations, what some of the obstacles are that that character has to overcome, etc. Once students have written nine scenarios about their character, they share their ideas with their team of peer responders to get audience feedback. Usually there are three other team members. The author reads aloud several scenarios to the team and the team offers written response to such prompts as "Your character could . . ." or "I think your character needs to . . . ," or "What would happen if your character did . . ." Once this has been completed, the stu-dents can use the scenarios as part of their story or can use them as a lead off point to start the process. The actual writing of the short story takes about four weeks. Students struggle with names for characters, obstacles to overcome, and solutions to prob-lems. As students are writing, I spend time doing one-on-one student/teacher conferences to get a feel for the growth of the story as well as the student writer. (1–2)

To keep track of what they discuss during the conference and to assess progress, Jane's students complete a form that guides them through the conference (Figure 2.2).

Figure 2.2 Creative Writing: Short Story Conference Sheet

Writer _____ Date _____ Period _____

Character Name _____

Type of Character _____

Major Conflict _____

What do you like about your character at this point? _____

_____

What do you think needs to be done to make your character more realistic? _____

_____

What other things can you tell me about your short story? _____

_____

What are some of the possible solutions you have explored for your short story? _____

_____

What can I do to help you at this point? _____

_____

Some teachers have their students prepare for the student/teacher conference by peer-conferencing with their classmates. In addition to the benefits of receiving feedback from fellow writers, Matt Kusic (1996), a student at Hempfield Area High School, revealed that the benefits of peer evaluation flow in both directions: "Peer evaluation . . . gives me the opportunity to read other students' writing." Jane Cowden (1996) gives her students at Big Spring High School in Newville, Pennsylvania, a list of expectations to use in preparation for their end-of-the-marking-period student/teacher conference (Figure 2.3).

Figure 2.3   Conference Expectations

End-of-Marking-Period Conferences: What I will expect you to review with me.

Your portfolio: What does it show about your growth as a writer? Is your cover sheet completed? Are you missing anything? If so, why?

Your completed compositions, other than those in your portfolio: Remember, the grand total of MNs should be at least 18.

Your records: The completed readings sheet, the completed compositions sheet, the individual progress sheets (if you haven't already turned them in). Are you keeping up on record-keeping?

Your goals sheet: How are you progressing? Will you reach your goals? Do they need to be modified?

Self-selected books: How many have you completed? How many gold cards have you written? How many book talks have you given?

Learning logs: Is your log always complete? (The required number per week? The required entries: one on reading, one on peer work? Two reader responses: a peer and a "trusted adult"?) Have you turned in your log on time? Every time? Have you done extra entries?

Required letters: Two sets of three letters to me in your portfolio (mid-marking period, end-of-marking period), letter to me on e-mail project, two sets of three reader responses to your peers' portfolio selections (mid-marking period, end-of-marking period), one or two e-mail letters to your correspondents.

Required writings: Have you completed the Chaucer-style poem, the Chaucer paper, the *Glass Menagerie* paper, the Beowulf/Arthur paper, the entries in your learning log on the Medieval period?

Classroom deportment: Cooperation, participation, collaboration: Have you conducted yourself appropriately in class? Have you come to class prepared and on time? Have you had excellent attendance? Have you done your share of the work during group activities? Have you helped others with their work? Have you never distracted your classmates? Have you always used class wisely?

Additional work: Have you done anything above and beyond the requirements? Are there any extra efforts or work you've done that you'd like me to consider before giving you a grade?

Grade: Based on the above information, what grade do you honestly believe you've earned this marking period?

Jane Blystone has the students work together at the editing stage.

> Once a short story is completed, the students participate in peer editing. Each student asks three students who are not on his/her team to read the story and give written feedback. The Short Story Peer Editor's Sheet (Figure 2.4) is duplicated so that every student has three copies to give to his/her peer editors. When the three readers have completed their responses, the author is free to return to the computer to revise the story based on ideas that these readers have recorded. This is audience awareness in action. As students move through this process, I see them going back to the peer editors for more explanations, and I also see trust being built between student reader and student writer. It becomes a close community that is very protective. (2–3)

Jane's students are learning to assess each other and themselves.

Figure 2.4 Short Story Peer Editor's Sheet

Writer ———————————— Date ———— Period ————

Peer Editor ———————————————— Edit # ————

What do you like about the main character? What are some weaknesses that the writer could work on to improve this character or make this character more realistic? ————————————

What do you think needs to be done to make the problem (conflict) clearer to the reader? ————————————

What things in the plot or setting might the writer need to revise to improve this story? ————————————

What are some of the possible solutions you think the writer might explore for this short story? _____

_____

What else do you think could be done to make this a well-written short story? Be specific. _____

_____

After Jane's students have completed their peer review and self-assessment process, including submitting their documents to spell checkers and grammar checkers on the computer if they wish, Jane asks them to engage in a day of peer editing. "Actually, it is a proofreading process," Jane admits, "because, as I tell the kids, computers can help you, but they don't catch everything—especially homonyms." Peer proofreaders use the Creative Writing: Short Story Editing Sheet (Figure 2.5) as a scoresheet. Her students call this sheet the "Red Pen" because it reminds them of earlier experiences with English and because Jane has it printed on "rocket red" paper to make a point. A student who receives a 4 or below (out of a possible 6) on the sheet raises a red flag, meaning he or she must have another conference with Jane to assess what strategies might improve the piece. Jane says that she never writes on the students' papers in this step, although students may write on each other's papers, with permission.

Figure 2.5 Creative Writing: Short Story Editing Sheet

Writer _____ Date _____ Period _____

Peer Editor _____

6 = superior   5 = excellent   4 = good
3 = fair   2 = poor   1 = unacceptable

Higher Order Concerns
___Focus—Define and illustrate (what is specific topic, what it isn't)
___Details/development—by examples; showing, not telling
___Organization—a logical order
___Voice—definition, why is it important? What is appropriate?

Middle Order Concerns
___Run-on sentences
___Subject-verb agreement
___Vocabulary—general wording
___Clichés—avoid phrases and words like *really, very, a lot*
___Verbs—forms of the verb *to be*; passive voice, *got*
___Pronoun-antecedent agreement
___Vague pronouns and unclear references
___Dangling modifiers
___Parallel construction in sentences
___Wordiness
___Sentence variety—the four types, different lengths,
      different openings

Lower Order Concerns
___Apostrophes—possessives and contractions
___Quotations
___Spelling
___Punctuation—commas, semicolons, end marks
___Capitalization

Jane's students become very sensitive to the idea of granting permission to write and comment on each other's papers. Even Ray Bradbury's friends wait for him to invite their comments. "One day when we were in full swing with this assessment process," Jane says, "a student who was not a member of our class came into the computer lab. She tried to read over another student's shoulder and the student editor blurted out, 'You'll have to ask the author's permission to read this'" (3) and proceeded to point out which classmate was the author. And it's not only the students who must obey this courtesy. "On another occasion," Jane continues, "an administrator dropped

42

by to see what the students were doing. He stopped at a computer to read over a ninth-grader's shoulder. The student said, very respectfully, 'Please don't read over my shoulder; I'll show it to you when I am finished,' which she did."

Jane's students realize that assessment means sharing.

> I used to let every student read their final draft before the whole class, but because the classes are so large, I have had to limit the number of pages in the short story and the number of students who read their stories to the class. . . . But each student reads his or her seven to ten page short story to their peer response team, and the team decides which story to share with the class. . . . When all stories have been read, I collect them to read, and I write narratives on 4 x 6 Post-it notes to each student about their work. This gives them one more opportunity to revise before they put together their portfolios. This is also the only time they get written feedback from me. (5)

Technology Supports Discussion

Some teachers make use of computer facilities to supplement their conferencing. The networking capabilities of computers allows teachers, such as our colleague Danette DiMarco (1997) at Slippery Rock University, to maintain "face-to-face" student/teacher and peer conferencing in the classroom while employing e-mail and "asynchronous environments, like listservs [circulating e-mail to those on a distribution list] and public posting domains," for peer response outside the classroom.

Danette sees her students moving from a sense of writing as a private enterprise to a face-to-face sharing of public writing with a small group of classmates, to a broader discussion of their writing by presenting it to "an on-line writing environment, where they are able to provide and receive feedback from a wider writing community." Typically her students would engage in peer response discussions in class and then post "on-line responses to a designated number of works" to the interactive environment, the electronic bulletin board. The students would then be assigned to read and "evaluate a grouping of the responses written by their peers of others' posted works" by posting their own written assessments of what they find. Danette reminds her students that "everyone deserves to receive an equal response." Danette feels that integrating "traditional classroom peer group strategies" with "technology-based responses enables students to understand peer response as a type or genre of composition that, in and of itself, necessitates oral as well as written response." Danette completes the cycle by returning to the classroom to evaluate the post-and-respond process in writing and through whole class discussion.

Progress Reports

Keeping track of conferences and student progress can be daunting. Kathy Kelly-Garris (1993), an English teacher at Penn-Trafford High School in Harrison City, Pennsylvania, uses a modified version of Nancie Atwell's (1987) "Status of the Class" to help with management and organization. The progress report form, a matrix that lists the names of the students down one side and the days of the week across the top, is placed on each front desk of a row at the beginning of class. Unlike Atwell's procedure, Kathy's students, not the teacher, fill out the form, telling her their plans for that day, "from drafting to conferencing to editing to finishing a final copy. If a student is peer conferencing that day, she must mark down who her partner will be. If a student wants a conference with [her teacher], she writes that on the form." Kathy describes her process:

> I collect the form and keep it with me as I circulate the room. I add minor notes on the form, indicating whether or not the student was on task. I believe that giving the students the responsibility of choosing what they'll be working on for the day reinforces the student-centeredness of the classroom. . . . Another use of this form is to keep track of time on task. I keep the daily . . . reports on file in order to see any patterns. To keep a record of academic progress, I use a steno pad to take notes about each

piece of writing the student has been working on. Each class member has a page in the steno pad and it is in this pad that I make notes about an individual student's progress. I rate the effectiveness of the conference using a check, check plus, or check minus. The rating is more of an assessment of my effectiveness during the conference as I try to determine how much I have helped the writer. Next, I make written notes about the writer's progress. I mark what the student does well, and I also mark what needs to be improved. In a later conference, I check to see if any progress has been made in that area. I never try to fix everything in the piece. I just give suggestions and ask questions.

Since it is difficult to remember each writer's work, the steno pad acts as a way for me to remember areas in which each writer excels or is in need of support. The pad also gives me freedom, since I am not tied to an excessive amount of record keeping; I am responsible for one record while the students are responsible for two—a writing folder [and a contents list, placed] on the inside flap of their manila folder, [containing] the title of each piece, date started, and date completed. Consequently, the students keep the nuts-and-bolts records, and I keep the maintenance record. Giving students responsibility lessens my time filling out forms and gives me more time to spend conferencing with students. (48–50)

Connie Fleeger, an English teacher at Karns City Area High School, allows her students plenty of choice when it comes to reading selections and group work, but she also demands responsibility from the students. For example, in her Shakespeare unit, after the class has read *Hamlet* together, she allows students to form groups and choose a play to study and present to their classmates. As students are clustered in various areas around the room (some in the hallway and some gathered around the teacher's desk), reading, discussing, and organizing, a member from each group must act as reporter and turn in a progress sheet, listing the group leader and members who were present and participating that day and what the group did with their time. Connie believes in freedom with accountability.

Checklists

Checklists are teacher-created instruments that are usually little more than a listing of traits that the teacher, students, and curriculum have decided are desirable for a specific subject or task. In addition to assessing products or artifacts of learning, checklists can be used to record observable student behaviors that are predetermined as desirable by both teacher and students. The teacher, acting as observer, looks for evidence of such traits as he or she works with students in the community of the classroom. Checklists are helpful only if the teacher can quickly record observations while working with students. To be time saving, checklists need to be simple and to the point, requiring a minimum of writing on the teacher's part. The purpose of these assessment instruments is to keep the teacher focused on what is important and provide a record of student growth from information gathered over a period of time, much the way that Kathy Kelly-Garris' progress reports do. Checklists are particularly helpful during cooperative learning projects, group presentations, and class discussions. Some teachers like to keep checklists on a clipboard, as suggested with peel-off labels, making them easily portable from group to group or from student to student.

Checklist assessment techniques can be used only in classrooms where teachers have opportunities to observe and students have opportunities to assume responsibility for their learning. For example, a teacher in an English classroom may want to keep track of writing behaviors that are important for development in composition. As students are working on drafts, conferencing, revising, or editing, the teacher may be watching for evidence of the students' understanding of the writing process. If so, a checklist like that found in Figure 2.6 may be helpful.

By using this type of checklist, the teacher and student will be able to easily pick up where they left off at the next confer-

Figure 2.6 Writing Conference Checklist (Cumulative)

STUDENT'S NAME (Title of Work)	DATE	FOCUS/THESIS	ORGANIZATION	TRANSITIONS	SENTENCE STRUCTURE	CONCLUSION	MECHANICS	COMMENTS
Susan B. (Questions)	3/21	+	+	✓	✓	—	+	work with Mark on conclusion
Mark R. (A Quiet Thought)	3/21	+	+	—	—	+	✓	good ideas - help with structure
Laura M. (Through My Eyes)	3/23	✓	✓	✓	✓	NA	—	early stages - still very rough
Jason P. (Justice)	3/19	+	+	—	✓	✓	—	
Nathan M. (Walk to the Beat)	3/20	+	+	+	+	✓	✓	working on conclusion
Kelly D. (Animal Protection)	3/21	✓	✓	—	✓	—	—	feels strongly about this topic
Greg W. (Untitled)	3/23	+	✓	—	✓	✓	✓	

Symbol explanations: + well developed
✔ satisfactory
– needs attention
NA not applicable

ence. For example, after the conference on March 21, the teacher and Susan know that she needs to work on the conclusion of her piece and check for ways to make transitions and sentence structure clearer. At the next conference, her teacher will be able to immediately identify the areas on which Susan was working.

Checklists can be devised by teachers or by teachers and students together. Often their use is simply one of organization and communication. Writing teachers often supply students with editing checklists that can be kept in writing folders and used by students as a reference when a piece gets to this stage of the process. Content-area teachers often use checklists that support the process of individualized, group, or discovery learning. Kimberly McWherter, science teacher at Derry Area High School in Pennsylvania, has her students use a checklist when writing up their laboratory experiments (see Figure 2.7). Such a checklist helps students double-check their assignments before handing them in. There are no gradations of quality on such a list, its purpose being one of organization rather than one of evaluation. However, gradations of quality could be added to the checklist, making it similar to a rubric and appropriate for use as an evaluative tool.

Figure 2.7   Laboratory Reports Checklist

	Included	
	Yes	*No*

FORMAT/MECHANICS
  1. Typed/word processed
  2. All sections of report included and in proper sequence
  3. Proper punctuation/grammar/spelling
  4. Written in third person

ORGANIZATION
  1. Ideas are easy to follow
  2. Well thought out

ABSTRACT
  1. Main point to be tested/learned is addressed
  2. Hypothesis is testable

INTRODUCTION
  1. Sufficient background information is included
  2. Usage of any appropriate equations is explained

MATERIALS
  Referenced with exceptions

PROCEDURES
  Referenced with exceptions

OBSERVATIONS
  1. In paragraph form
  2. Complete (no quantities)

	Included	
	Yes	No

DATA
1. Neat/well organized
2. Complete. Includes all appropriate info.
3. Tables/graphs have titles
4. Units included

CALCULATIONS
1. Neat/organized
2. Easy to follow
3. Sample calculations of all types included
4. Units included

CONCLUSION
1. Abstract supported/not supported
2. Uses data effectively to justify conclusions
3. Applies ideas from lab to uses in business, industry, daily life.

Checklists may be used for assessment or for evaluative purposes—that is, they may be formative or summative. The checklist in Figure 2.6 would be used for assessment purposes, but teachers also use checklists, along with other assessment instruments, in order to evaluate student progress based on the data. An example of a summative checklist may be found in Figure 2.8. This type of checklist can be rather formal, as in the case of a checklist that is used in place of or along with report cards, or it can be informal and even filled out by the student and teacher together in order for the student to self-evaluate.

However, observation is only a part of data gathering. Like anyone else, teachers need to be careful not to jump to conclusions based on a few observations. Observations need to be documented and used as a part of a much larger picture.

Dialogue Discussion

We often hear teachers lament, "I have 125 students; how do I

Figure 2.8 Research Methods Checklist

Student's Name

	Does Not Appear	1 Minimal	2 Adequate	3 In Detail
A. *Discusses the Issue/Topic*				
Defines terms				
Makes connections				
B. *States the Overall Question Being Studied*				
A thesis				
C. *Timely Explanation of Reason for Constructing Questions*				
Why give a survey				
D. *States Method for Gathering the Data*				
Who was asked				
How they were chosen				
E. *Discusses the Responses*				
Significance of the statistical information				
Analysis of the responses				
F. *Draws Conclusions*				
Summarizes the findings				
Implications for further thought				
G. *Appendix Presentation*				
The questionnaire				
Interview questions				
Number of responses				
Table of responses				
H. *Overall Writing Quality*				
Well organized				
Mature sentence structure				
Free of mechanical error				
Interesting				

(One copy to be completed by the student and one copy by the instructor for discussion during a conference.)

know if they're really understanding what I'm trying to teach them? I'm not even really sure if they understand what I mean when I give them feedback on papers and tests." The obvious way to know what someone is thinking is to ask them. Unfortunately, it's not always possible to have individual discussions with our students. Yet, if we really want to assess their understanding of our feedback, we have to find a way to talk with them. Maureen Neal, of Mesa State College in Colorado, does this when she instigates "dialogue discussions" with her students when she hands back "corrected" papers. Maureen uses this dialogue to better understand what her students are thinking and doing, an invaluable tool for instruction. Maureen explains:

> In courses in which I can't use a portfolio system and must instead assign and grade single papers, I have tried to find ways to ensure that the comments I'm making are heard by students, and [dialogue response] is one of the ways I'm trying to do that. When I assign a paper or project, I include a grading scale as part of the prompt. Then, when I give back papers, I ask students to communicate with me in writing about the paper and its grade by,
>
> 1. telling me what they think I'm trying to say to them about the work (in other words, translate or interpret my comments) and,
>
> 2. responding to the comments and/or the grade by agreeing, disagreeing, asking questions, or answering my questions on the text. I also ask them to put in writing any questions they have about the grade or the grading process, or my thinking about the paper. We may send a paper back and forth several times before we end this conversation.
>
> This method . . . helps me to know whether or not the student actually reads my comments; it helps me to understand how much of my criticism is understood; and, it allows a student to verify compliments and positive comments as well as those more critical. It gives the student a voice and an active part in the grading process. [An example of Maureen's dialogue with a

Figure 2–9 Sample Page from Dialogue Discussion

own liking. Her mother doesn't understand the strategy behind the game, she only wants

Meimei to " win more, lose less" (1484). This control causes Meimei to lose interest in

the game she had fallen in love with. It was no longer important to her. It was no longer

fun. Although her parents gave her support and made many sacrifices for their daughter

such as moving her brother's bed into the living room, and allowing Meimei to leave her

bowl of food half-finished (1484), she seemed to feel unloved by her parents. They were

more interested in the game and less interested in the little girl.

2. Edith in "Reunion" tried not only being a mother to her son Brian but also to her

drunk of a husband, Jack. Edith asks Jack to "stay away from the whiskey for once

because everyone knows what happens when he drinks" (1547). She is always trying to

smooth things over for her husband, that Brian seems to get tossed to the side. How can

she have time for her little boy, when there is a big boy that wants all the attention for

3. himself. Even in playful moments while trying to figure out a signal to go home, "Edith

winks at Brian causing him to fling his torso over the front seat, wriggle his shoulders,

and giggle." But this is short-lived as she tells him to "mind your shirt buttons, or you'll

tear them off" (1549). Although Edith tries to help her son fit in with the other cousins at

the reunion, she is not very concerned about his feelings and what he wants. She just

wants him to "run along and play but to be careful not to get grass stains on his

pants"(1551). I feel that Edith is too caught up in what Jack will do next that she is

unaware of her child and his insecurities and worries. Edith is selfish in her views of

being a mother, she accuses Jack of " ruining her life" but doesn't consider that he is

ruining Brian's life also. She is caught up in her own worries and troubles.

52

student, Jami Zimmerman, can be seen by looking at a page from her paper (Figure 2.9).] Students do not always agree with my judgment, and they let me know that clearly. But by dealing with disagreements this way, I am much more able to respond to a student's complaints—partly because the complaint is made explicit, and partly because the process of writing back and forth is a kind of sharing of authority and energy in a way that office conversations/confrontations about grades are not. I also find that I can be much more rigorous in grading when I use this dialogue response system than when I do not use it, [though] I'm not sure why that is the case. (1997, 3)

Teachers can share ideas and formats with one another about the numerous forms and uses for anecdotal records, progress reports, interviews, checklists, and dialogues, but whatever the format for assessment by observation, teachers should be efficient and clear in their interpretation and evaluation of student growth.

Thoughts for Further Inquiry

1. Try being an observer for fifteen to twenty minutes. In a classroom, either yours or someone else's, record objectively what you are observing. Try to make these observations as descriptive as possible; remember, don't make judgments. Your role as observer is to collect data, so record what you see or hear without drawing conclusions.
2. Think of an assignment you've given as a teacher or received as a student. Devise a checklist that could be used as a formative assessment instrument. Think of what traits or procedures are important and how progress could be recorded.
3. Devise a survey you could use in the beginning of the school year. Think of information your students could share with you that would help drive your instruction. Can you devise a survey for the end of the school year that helps you assess the curriculum and your effectiveness as a teacher?

4. With others, discuss the pros and cons of peer conferencing. What can we do, as teachers, to support our students as they work with each other and how can we help them to provide useful feedback?

5. How can technology support our use of assessment? Share strategies we can use on-line for assessment or suggest computer programs that can help us devise instruments.

3

Strategies for Assessment and Evaluation

I will merely ask . . . of all the knowledge available in the world—which by the way, according to experts is doubling about every eighteen months—how can we have the audacity to determine an individual's entire future by the way in which that individual answers one, three, or twenty questions about a totally insignificant segment of all that knowledge?

—Peter Krause

Following a recent program evaluation at our university, we were perplexed by some of the recommendations an accrediting team made about a particular graduate course for Reading Certification, one that discusses detecting a reader's difficulties and setting up a plan of instruction based on that assessment. When we read the evaluation, the examiner recommended that we should "remove the reference to formal evaluations" in our syllabi, or "explain where such instruments are taught." The course examines various assessment strategies, ways to gather such assessments, evaluating and drawing conclusions, and reporting findings, including working with other teachers to implement instructional strategies. But because our students don't use some of the well-known traditional reading tests, which have been normed and standardized, the examiner assumed that we only taught "informal" evaluation. As we considered how to reply, we realized that the examiner didn't understand our definition of *formal* evaluation. Formal evaluations are much like conclusions drawn from qualitative research; they are based on a wealth of data, triangulated using various sources, and looked upon as possibilities and directions rather than concrete truths. However, they *are* formal in that they are organized, well-documented, and look to conclusions supported by data.

As part of the paradigm under which we work, we understand that evaluation is ongoing. As we teach, we constantly look to the students for evidence of growth, learning being organic and lifelong. We know that neither end-of-the-unit tests nor Scantron tests and graded homework assignments can meet all these criteria. The instruments we use to assess and evaluate are varied, appropriate in some cases and not needed in others. Unlike mandated, large-scale evaluation tools, such as SATs and state examinations, teachers and students need evaluation tools that support learning as well as measure it. Evaluation can be a help to students rather than an end-product; reporting can be a matter of sharing, celebrating, planning, and envisioning rather than just distributing scores for newspapers and politicians to judge schools, teachers, and students as "highest" or "lowest."

If we accept that assessment and evaluation must be more authentic, must drive instruction, and must help students understand what they know and set goals for future learning, then the inevitable problem is how to accomplish authentic assessment and evaluation. At various inservice workshops, teachers hear about rubrics and checklists, and portfolios and performance assessments, but it's difficult to know where and when to begin.

A Rose by Any Other Name

Definitions *are* important. Sometimes just trying to define what we're talking about is a necessary first step. Terms such as alternative assessment, authentic assessment, and performance assessment are frequently and mistakenly used interchangeably. *Alternative assessment*, a term popularized by Grant Wiggins (1989a), is a broad term referring to any type of assessment that deviates from the traditional, behavioral, stimulus-response model typified by one-answer, multiple-choice tests found on teacher-created tests and standardized examinations. *Authentic assessment* refers to tasks that are real and meaningful to the learner in today's world. *Performance assessment*, which may be authentic as well as alternative, refers to any type of assessment that provides opportunities for students to demonstrate what they know, putting what they have learned into a meaningful context and showing what they know.

Alternative Assessment

Many teachers today, especially those who are working to make their classrooms student centered and provide authentic learning tasks, have moved away from testing—for some very good reasons. For many, their educational preparation consisted of being taught the virtues of multiple-choice tests of content knowledge, struggling to write questions with answers that will be "accurate, relevant, and of the most appropriate scope in relation to the other answer choices" (Popham 1988, 142)—in other words, satisfied by "only one right answer." Even today preservice teachers around the country are taught how to write such tests in colleges of education. Such teaching is still validated by professional test-makers who assemble examinations that affect students and schools all over the country. These state- and nationally mandated tests sacrifice validity for reliability. As Wiggins (1993) points out, "test-makers generally end up being more concerned with the precision of scores than with the intellectual value of the challenge. Thus the forms of testing and scoring used are indirect and generic, designed to minimize the ambiguity of tasks and answers" (202).

"To assume that tests should assess whether all students everywhere have the same 'knowledge' is to short-circuit a vital educational dialogue in a pluralistic and diverse society. Genuine intellectual performance," says Wiggins, "is inherently personalized, and the meanings, strengths, and aspirations that we derive from an education are inherently idiosyncratic" (202). Testing, however, needn't be so narrowly defined. Although Barbara King-Shaver (1992) and her English department colleagues at South Brunswick High School in New Jersey had changed their views of teaching and learning dramatically over the years, their final exams had not reflected that change. Therefore, they began looking for alternatives to the traditional final exams they had been giving, hoping to find "an assessment method that would more accurately reflect [their] English classrooms during the year."

"We began . . . by identifying what it is our students do in their English classes," Barbara says. "During the year, our students read and analyze literature through self-reflection and class discussion. They also write about literature, using the writing process and peer editing. Our students construct and reconstruct meaning, using reading, speaking, listening, and writing. We were looking for a method of assessment that mirrored these activities." Barbara discovered teachers who used a process-based examination, one that "occurs over a number of days in a familiar, friendly setting." The schedule went along the following lines:

Day 1 is a focused freewriting, an individual activity whose objective is generating ideas. On this day, students freewrite about a given topic. Following the freewriting, students meet in small groups and share their responses. The writing is collected and a folder is begun for each student.

Day 2 is a reading day, a small group activity whose objective is discussion. On this day, the class reads a story, poem, essay, or excerpt from a novel that is related to the topic of the previous day's freewriting. Students share their initial observations of the work in small groups, attempting to arrive at some consensus on what is happening in the work (theme, use of language, etc.).

Students may take notes during their discussion, and all their notes are added to the folder and collected.

Day 3 is another reading day, this time an individual activity whose objective is drafting. On this day students individually reread the work presented on the previous day and make additional notes if necessary. A writing topic is given, and students are then invited to write an essay on a topic related to the work of literature they read and discussed. Students begin drafting their papers, and they have use of all the notes in their folders. All their work is collected at the end of class and placed into their folders.

Day 4 is revising, an individual/group activity whose objective is editing. Folders are given back to students for revising and editing, and students work with peers for revision and editing comments. At the end of the day, their folders are collected.

Day 5 is both revising/editing, an individual activity whose objective is writing a final draft. After the final drafts are completed, the folders are collected and assessed.

The number of days may vary, depending on the length of the work read and the length of class periods. Teachers may decide on a schedule ahead of time and fit the process examination into this schedule. For example, with short class periods, two days may be given for revising and editing, although the students' work is collected each day. (6)

Barbara and her colleagues were attracted to the process-based examination because it "tested composition and literature—the areas we wanted to test. . . . Two aspects of the process-based model that we felt were important, aspects not included in the traditional final exam, were the peer discussion groups before writing and peer editing groups after writing. The use of peer input directly reflects what our students do all year as they read and write. It also supports our belief in collaborative learning and the making of meaning as a communal activity" (6).

Barbara explains how the process-based model of final examinations is applied to a specific course:

Seniors in a World Literature class begin their exam process on Monday by reading the short story "Disappearing," a tale about a wife who is overweight and tries to disappear because both she and her husband are unhappy with her body. She takes up dieting and swimming, becoming obsessed with losing weight. The wife becomes thinner and thinner, pushing herself to lose even more weight. She hopes one day to become so thin that she can disappear into the water.

After reading the story individually, the students break into small groups to discuss the literal and figurative interpretation of the text and discuss how the ideas presented in the text parallel other works read during the year or how the ideas present an observation on the ideas in another work. During the small group discussions, students may take notes.

Many of the students writing about "Disappearing" take the theme of transformation, for example, and apply it to characters in works they have read, noting a physical change in Gregor in "Metamorphosis," an emotional change in Gertrude in Hamlet, and a psychological change in the lawyer in *The Bet*.

At home, students are told to choose one idea that emerged from their group discussion or occurred to them individually. They are expected to begin drafting an essay that will discuss the story and will use at least three works read during the year to further illustrate their points.

On Tuesday, students meet with a peer editor to obtain feedback for revising and editing their papers. The students take turns serving as peer editors for each other. The peer editing comments are written down and attached to the draft. On Wednesday, the students write a second draft, using their peer feedback as needed, and on Thursday, they prepare their final draft, attaching peer comments and previous drafts. (7)

Even though Barbara King-Shaver and her colleagues believe that process-based exams help their students be successful, there are still some constraints and artificial elements. "For one thing," Barbara says, "the text needs to be short enough (two to three pages) for students to read and respond to within the time frame. This length text is not always easy to find." Another constraint is the teacher's role. Although Barbara doesn't "intervene in the reading, discussing, and writing components of the assessment," she believes "the teacher should provide a supportive environment" (7).

Once teachers begin to question behaviors that accompany traditional testing, other alternatives such as Barbara's will be developed. Teachers will begin to reject the obsession with test security (protecting exams as though they were the Academy Awards), time limits ("fifteen minutes remain . . ."), artificial deadlines, and a belief that individual performance is a virtue superior to collaboration.

Constructing Tests: Criteria for Authenticity

There was a time when we would have thought that *authentic testing* was an oxymoron. Traditionally, testing referred to known-answer questions, even when asked in essay form. Questions that asked students to discuss symbolism in *Moby Dick* or describe the causes of post-colonial expansion or argue the point that slavery had little or everything to do with the Civil War are still known-answer questions, asking students to display their powers of memory and retention.

Before we test, we need to reconsider what learning is. If learning is accumulating discrete bits of information, then multiple-choice testing makes sense. Wiggins, however, suggests that our goal in education is to help students become more than passive receptors of info-bites and become "intellectual performers" who make the knowledge their own in a context that is useful in the world.

Authentic assessment refers to tasks that are real and meaningful to the learner in today's world. Wiggins (1993) suggests that skills and knowledge be assessed in school the same way as they are in the "real" world. The assignments should be "either replicas of or analogous to the kinds of problems faced by adult citizens and consumers or professionals in the field" (206).

Second and Third Story Thinking

When constructing tests, teachers must look at how they are asking students to demonstrate what they know. The phrasing of test items in teacher-constructed tests was divided into three categories by Bellanca and Fogarty (1991): gathering, processing, and applying. These categories were distinguished by the verbs used to direct the students. The verbs told not only what was being asked of the students, but how much was being asked of them.

The *gather* category, the first category, involved little more than recall and made use of verbs such as *describe, count, match, name, recite, select,* and *tell*. At this stage students were asked to gather what they knew and regurgitate it. The *process* category included test questions that made use of words like *compare, sort, reason, construct, solve, distinguish, explain, classify, analyze,* and *inform*. The *apply* category used words like *evaluate, imagine, judge, predict, speculate, apply, estimate,* and *forecast*.

Bellanca and Fogarty borrowed from the thinking of Oliver Wendell Holmes, who represented the thinking process as a three-story building: "There are one-story intellects, two-story intellects, and three-story intellects with skylights. All fact collectors who have no aim beyond their facts are one-story men. Two-story men compare, reason, generalize, using the labors of fact collectors as well as their own. Three-story men idealize, imagine, predict—their best illumination comes from above, through the skylight." Bellanca and Fogarty imposed their three categories of gathering, processing, and applying onto Holmes' three-story intellects and created a house whose floors were decorated with the appropriate verbs and with stairs leading up to higher levels, featuring a skylight for good measure.

Some teachers have discovered that a test to demonstrate

what a student knows involves issues such as choice, research, creativity, and time. Jim's brother, Donald Strickland, an English teacher at Penfield High School in Rochester, New York, has designed an English curriculum that supports the social studies curriculum through literature selections and writing opportunities. Don and the social studies teacher use a combined project to evaluate their students' learning in the two classes, and the project or the final test examines not only the students' knowledge of social studies but also their ability to communicate what they know and their view of the world (the purpose of writing). Figure 3.1 is the assignment that the students receive in this eleventh-grade English/social studies class.

Figure 3.1   American Studies Final Project

This project is your chance to show the class and the teachers your ability to select, research, comprehend, synthesize, organize and present material on a topic of your choosing. It will be worth 50 percent of your English final exam grade and 50 percent of your social studies final exam grade.

Assignment:
- Identify a trend, issue, theme, process, practice, or idea in both the nineteenth and twentieth centuries (e.g., immigration issues, ethnicity, concepts of democracy, gender equity, the public's response to government action or inaction, etc.).
- Compare the status of this trend, etc., at a given point in each century (e.g., public acceptance of the Mexican-American War vs. the Vietnam War).
- Delineate the similarities from the differences across the two centuries.
- Analyze the causes and conditions which account for these similarities and differences.
- Present your findings in an appropriate form.

The project has optional forms. It could be a written paper; it could be point/counterpoint oral presentation; it could be comparative pieces of historical fiction; it could be a debate between two historical characters; or another format designed by you, the student.

Learning outcomes:
1. The student will explore and consider a number of possible areas in history to select the subject of the project. [This step should be accomplished by February 12–16.]
2. The student will engage in discussions with peers or teachers to refine subject, scope, and form of the project. [Each student should schedule a teacher's conference during the week of April 8–12.]
3. The student will engage in independent research and study to immerse himself/herself in the historical domain he/she has selected.
4. The student will synthesize his/her own perspective or point of view on the subject selected.
5. The student will organize the information and analysis in an appropriate fashion.
6. The student will write and present the material in a manner which best demonstrates his/her mastery of the historical principles involved and ability to synthesize original points of view.
[The presentations will be scheduled during the week of June 3–7.]
Note! The deadlines cited in steps 1 and 2 are mandatory. Any student who does not meet these interim deadlines will have points deducted from the overall score.

Don and the class discuss the assignment, ensuring that words such as *delineate* and *analyze* are clear, although this type of thinking and writing is not new to the students in these classes. The form of their answer is optional; some students write a paper that is rather traditional while others choose to create video productions or perform oral presentations, re-enactments, skits, and debates. The students are not only allowed choice, they are encouraged to be creative and use demonstrations that will engage their audience, a rather authentic task. The outcomes listed as part of the directions help students plan their time but still leave them ultimately responsible. Since a traditional test is a culmination of the course or unit of study, the grading of a final test leaves no opportunity for teaching. In this case, however, the teacher is not waiting to evaluate a product at the end. Instead, the teacher supports the students throughout the project through conferencing, and the opportunities for teaching present themselves during the process. Along with the instructions for this test and the explanation of outcomes and due dates, the students in these classes are presented with guidelines that clearly explain how the final exam project will be evaluated (Figure 3.2). With a clear explanation of what is expected and required, students can use the guidelines throughout the project for peer-assessment and self-assessment before they are used by their teacher as an evaluative tool.

Figure 3.2   American Studies Final Project Rubric

Analysis:
4
- The proposition demonstrates serious, original thought and judgment.
- The proposition involves a specific comparison of two points in American history, one from the 19th and one from the 20th century.
- The proposition is analytical rather than merely informative.
- The issue or proposition is clearly and compellingly stated.

3
- The proposition demonstrates serious thought and judgment.
- The proposition involves a general comparison between two points in American history, one from the 19th and one from the 20th century.
- The proposition is primarily analytical, but is, to some degree, informative.
- The issue or proposition is clearly and compellingly stated.

2
- The proposition demonstrates a familiar point of view or judgment.
- The proposition involves an overly general comparison between two points in American history.
- The proposition is primarily informative.
- The proposition is clearly stated.

1
- The proposition demonstrates a familiar point of view or judgment.

- The proposition involves an overly general comparison between two points in American history.
- The proposition is merely informative.
- The proposition is left unstated or unfocused.

Presentation:
4
- The attention of the audience is commanded.
- Language is clear and fluent.
- Technology and/or visual aids strongly enhance communication of the main idea.
- Oral presentations refer to notes but are not primarily read from a script.

3
- The attention of the audience is held.
- Language is clear and fluent.
- Technology and/or visual aids support communication of the main idea.
- Oral presentations refer to notes but are not primarily read from a script.

2
- The attention of the audience is occasionally lost.
- Language is usually clear, but sometimes awkward.
- Technology and/or visual aids add little to the communication of the main idea.
- Oral presentations are primarily read directly from a script.

1
- The attention of the audience is never really gained.
- Language is stilted and awkward.
- Technology and/or visual aids inhibit or detract from the communication of the main idea.
- Oral presentations are entirely limited to a script.

Content:
4
- Familiarity and facility with the people, events, laws, government, culture, etc., that create the trends, issues . . . used in the comparison are demonstrated.
- The comparison cited is clearly balanced and unforced. It comes

from an even-handed presentation of factual material.
- The project illustrates in a sophisticated manner how the trend, issue . . . is significant to the time period cited.
- Points used to support the thesis are substantive, well-researched and well-developed.

3

- Familiarity and some facility with the people, events, laws, government, culture, etc., that create the trends, issues . . . used in the comparison are demonstrated.
- The comparison cited is primarily balanced and unforced. It comes from an even-handed presentation of factual material.
- The project illustrates in a competent manner how the trend, issue . . . is significant to the time period cited.
- Points used to support the thesis are concrete, appropriately researched, and adequately developed.

2

- Awareness of the people, events, laws, government, culture, etc., that create the trends, issues . . . used in the comparison is demonstrated.
- The comparison cited is somewhat unbalanced or forced. It comes from an occasionally distorted presentation of factual material.
- The project illustrates in an inconsistent manner how the trend, issue . . . is significant to the time period cited.
- Points used to support the thesis are presented, but are under-researched and under-developed.

1

- An inconsistent or inaccurate awareness of the people, events, laws, government, culture, etc., that create the trends, issues . . . used in the comparison is demonstrated.
- The comparison cited is unbalanced and forced. It comes from a distorted presentation of factual material.
- The project never illustrates how the trend, issue . . . is significant to the time period cited.
- Points used to support the thesis are presented, but show no evidence of research and are largely undeveloped.

Research:
4
- Primary sources are predominantly used.

67

- Sources are used to achieve both depth and breadth of analysis.
- A large variety of sources and/or techniques (such as interviews, electronic sources, etc.) are used.
- Solid evidence is given of having independently used sources outside of the traditional ones (college and university, museums, personal correspondence, etc.).

3

- Some primary sources are used, but primarily secondary sources are used.
- Sources are used to achieve some depth and breadth of analysis.
- Sources of basically the same type are used.
- Sources that are outside of the traditional ones are used, with assistance.
- Libraries other than the school or town library are used (college and university, museums, etc.).

2

- Only secondary sources and/or textbook materials are used.
- Sources are used to achieve a superficial level of coverage (information).
- Ongoing assistance is required to locate materials.
- Bibliography and documentation is inadequately or incorrectly done.

1

- Sources are encyclopedic, undocumented, or personal knowledge.
- Sources are used to provide limited coverage of the topic.
- Documentation is missing.

Mechanics:
2

- Paragraphing is appropriate and consistent.
- Topic sentences are primarily judgmental in nature, rather than factual. Each makes a point that supports and extends the thesis proposition.
- Organizational structure is clearly evident and consistently followed.
- Grammar is accurate and consistent. Some minor errors may be evident.
- Documentation of sources is accurate and consistent. Bibliography is complete and accurate. Form is correct and consistent. Some minor errors may be present.

1.5

One of the above descriptors is not present.

1

Two of the above descriptors are not present.

.5

- Paragraphing is inconsistent.
- Topic sentences are primarily factual in nature. Some are not focused on the thesis proposition.
- Organizational structure is rarely evident.
- Grammar is inconsistent. Some major errors or a number of minor errors may be evident.
- Documentation of sources is inconsistent or incomplete. Bibliography is incomplete or inaccurate. Form is inconsistently followed. Some major errors may be present.

Using tests like this one gives students a chance to "do history" and to "do English" instead of just regurgitating facts. These assessments help students see a purpose for history, reading, and writing, and give them an opportunity to use their interests and talents in conjunction with knowledge they have learned in the content areas. If learning is to be authentic, teachers will need to give students opportunities to use authentic means of demonstrating what they have learned. Rather than having students pick answers or do a quick "dumping" of all they know about a topic in forty-four minutes, we need to "ask the student to *justify* answers or choices" (Wiggins 1993, 206). We need to think of ongoing testing where students are asked follow-up questions to answers. Wiggins says that this type of test offers "concurrent feedback and the possibility of self-adjustment during the test" (206). One authentic test adults face is a job interview. Questions are prepared in advance but interviewees are asked to justify answers and asked questions based on their previous answers. This is an example of an organic test situation. Just as the job interviewer, teachers should be looking for "consistency of student work—the assessment of *habits* of mind in performance" (207).

Ralph Feather, a high school science teacher from Derry Area Schools in Pennsylvania, gives his geology students an opportunity to demonstrate what they have learned in an authentic test with questions that deal with real-life issues—building a highway, installing a swimming pool, fencing in a yard (Figure 3.3). Not only will Ralph be able to determine who can apply the information taught in class, the students themselves can see that their knowledge can solve real-world problems.

Figure 3.3 Geology Exam

Geology Exam	Name:_____
Chapter 9: Mass Wasting	Date:_____PD:_____

In each of the following problems, read what is expected and determine if the proposed items should be built and note any mitigation needed to be successful.

1. You have been hired to study the area mapped below for a possible route for a new four-lane highway. How would you go about planning the highway and what mitigation might be required for a successful project?

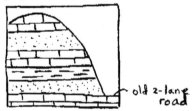

2. Mr. and Mrs. Pool have decided to put a pool in their backyard. Study the cross-section of their backyard and decide whether a pool could be placed in the yard with or without mitigation.

3. List and describe any dangers the directors of the private school shown below might encounter due to mass wasting.

4. The Picket family is planning to put up a wall-fence and change the grade of the land around their home to reduce possible mass wasting problems. What limitations, if any, might they run into and what mitigation, if any, will be required in order to do as they plan?

Test Is Not Necessarily
a Four-Letter Word

Performance assessment offers students ways to perform with knowledge, ways in which they can demonstrate what they have learned by combining the skills and knowledge acquired through course content with their prior and distinct knowledge of the world. Tests are admittedly one way to do this, but teachers must know how to provide opportunities in tests where students "do" science or history or language or philosophy. This is performance.

Many think of performance assessment as portfolio exhibition, demonstrations, presentations, or artistic models, but it can be even broader than this. Grant Wiggins (1993) explains that even testing can be a form of performance assessment if the tests are designed in a way to afford learners opportunities to connect, explain, and demonstrate their content knowledge.

When constructing performance-assessment tests, teachers should be careful to ask students to use their knowledge to produce something. The questions or problems posed on tests should mirror problems encountered in an authentic experience of the content area. Teachers should also remove artificial constraints to whatever degree possible in an educational setting. Rather than requiring tests to be completed in one seating or papers to be submitted at one deadline, the problem should be handled organically, developing with feedback. No one solves problems in a vacuum.

Joette Conger (1997), an English teacher at Downer's Grove High School in Illinois, gives her journalism students a performance-based final exam in addition to continuous authentic assignments throughout the semester. The Journalistic Writing final asks students to behave like journalists. The questions they face are ones that journalists face every day working under deadline. For example, one question that requires that they think like journalists poses the following situation (remember these students live just outside Chicago):

"The Chicago Bulls are approaching their record-breaking win-loss record. None of the major players is injured. Everyone expects the Bulls to win another championship. Everyone knows the record and the scores of all the games. Your assignment is to write a story for your local newspaper covering the last four games, which are scheduled 'away' games."

The students are not required to write the story; instead they're asked to describe their angle for the story, their focus, interviewees, and some of the questions. In other words, how does a journalist find a story when there is no apparent story? Another question asks them to actually write a feature story within the exam period; however, the students are made aware of the question well before the test date and are allowed to bring a draft with them if they've had the foresight to think ahead. Joette even allows collaboration on parts of the final.

During one part of the final, students are allowed to work together to write attention-getting headlines for each of the news articles distributed with the test. Each student must come up with a unique headline but they may work with each other in the process of creating their headlines.

Joette's students have practiced these activities in class and in assignments. The test asks them to perform in ways that they've rehearsed and in ways that mirror authentic situations.

Constraints of Testing

All assessments face constraints, the most common of which are time and resources. How much time should students have to complete a task, and what materials should be available to them? If we believe that the tasks we require of students should parallel real-life situations in the area being tested, then the time and resources allowed should be typical of an authentic situation.

Time, one of the more obvious constraints of traditional testing, can be addressed if teachers and students look at tests as processes or performances rather than "brain dumps" of everything students can recall. For example, Barbara King-Shaver's (1992) alternative to the traditional tests, process exams, allows a stretch of time for the test. A process exam in American Literature follows this schedule:

On the first day, students are given a one-page text, Faulkner's "Nobel Prize Acceptance Speech," to read in class. While reading, they are asked to record thoughts or questions they have in a reader response journal. The students share their responses and questions during a class discussion analyzing Faulkner's speech. The students may take notes.

On the second day, the writing assignment is introduced: The students are asked to discuss what Faulkner means when he describes literature as the "record of man" and "pillars to help him endure and prevail," and they are asked to apply these ideas to two works they have read during the year. The students are further asked to include at least one literary term studied to support their discussion. The students may use their reader response journals and class notes as they begin prewriting. All their work is collected at the end of class.

On the third day, the prewriting is handed back to the students, and they begin drafting their essays. Once again, all paperwork is collected at the end of class, to be returned on the fourth day when students will revise and edit their papers. . . .

The process-based examination reflects what occurs in English classes throughout the year. A process exam integrates reading and writing, supports the writing process, supports the reading process, supports collaborative learning, and supports a process approach to learning. In short, the process examination is authentic assessment because it reflects the collaborative reading and writing processes that people use in college, on the job, and in life. (7)

Writing tests are equally constrained. For instance, many standardized tests require a writing "sample" to be completed in a brief block of time, sometimes as little as thirty minutes (the Praxis exam, for example). Writers know that real writing, writing in which one hopes to demonstrate who one is as a writer, cannot be completed in thirty minutes. Other constraints are tied into the time restriction: writing about topics that mean little to the writer, those not of the writer's choosing, and those for which no opportunity has been provided to consider research. Needless to say, writing to such prompts does not demonstrate one's writing abilities and is therefore neither authentic nor performance assessment. Some school districts in places like Kentucky and Colorado do give student writers time—over class periods, over days—to draft, revise, and edit their pieces, to demonstrate their understanding of the process as well as their ability to write. However, it is more the case that teachers have to teach their students to deal with the constraints of time. Barbara King-Shaver (1992) feels "students should also experience shorter timed writing responses (a type of writing they may be asked to do on essay exams in college or on the AP exam)" (7), more to make the students test-wise than to use as an authentic evaluation. As with other types of timed writing responses, Barbara and her colleagues assign the topics in order to give the students practice responding to assignments not entirely of their own choosing.

Resources, both textual and human, almost always are constrained during testing situations for the convenience of the test-makers and to level the playing field. However, if the task or test is authentic, what would be the reason for keeping books and materials away from students ("Clear your desks except for paper and a pencil")? If teachers wish to measure student understanding, rather than play Trivial Pursuit, why not let students bring notes to a testing situation? Even some doctoral programs are easing constraints, allowing candidates to bring one note card to each comprehensive test—the ultimate final exam. Before making a diagnosis, don't doctors look up specifics and research? Before presenting a case, don't lawyers spend hours poring over texts and researching? Would anyone tell a lawyer he couldn't use his notes at a trial? Doesn't a good mechanic consult a manual or discuss a problem with a colleague before tackling a nonroutine problem with a car's engine? In school, such unconstrained practices would not only assess how students prepare, summarize, and identify important topics, but if our task is authentic, such resources would allow a student to tackle the task at hand—to demonstrate understanding of knowledge and skills in the context of an authentic task. Constraints in testing should mirror those constraints a task might have in a real situation. Kathleen gives an authentic final in her reading or language arts methods courses, distributed two weeks before exam week, and requires students to turn it in, word-processed, by the course's scheduled meeting time during final exam week. This is one of the prompts the students are given:

> You are being interviewed for a teaching position for a first-grade opening in an urban school district. You have explained

to the principal and panel of teachers who are interviewing you that you know the importance of a literate environment in an elementary classroom and that you believe that learning to read is a natural learning event. One of the interviewers then asks you, "Exactly *how* do children in your class learn to read? *How* do you teach reading? Do you believe children need phonics instruction?" What would be your response?

The test allows students to use any sources they feel are appropriate, and time to demonstrate what they know, supported by research; more important, it requires that they synthesize, explain, and support rather than regurgitate. The test's authenticity lies in the fact that most will soon be placed in a situation where their future career depends on their ability to answer such questions. Granted, in a real interview, they would be required to think on their feet, and they will be given a chance to practice that skill during their portfolio presentations. But for now, this type of test gives them a first chance to begin putting the pieces together. Some students have returned a year or two later to say how helpful it was to have had such an opportunity to collect their thoughts before being interviewed for a teaching position.

Scoring and Evaluating: Advantages of Using Rubrics

Even after teachers transform their assessment process to make it alternative, authentic, and/or performance based, their job has only begun. Those tests have to be scored, graded, and evaluated. The guidelines that Don Strickland (1996) uses for his English/American Studies final (see Figure 3.2) are valuable for both assessment and evaluation purposes. These guidelines are commonly referred to as rubrics, scoring tools that list both the criteria for an assignment (what needs to be addressed or demonstrated) and an articulation of the quality of the student achievement for the criteria. A rubric is a tool that can drive instruction as well as evaluate performance.

Teachers and students find rubrics to be useful and "friendly" tools for both teaching and assessment. Says Terrie St. Michel (1997) of South Mountain High School in Phoenix,

> Every assignment should include a rubric—clearly stated criteria by which the assignment will be evaluated and graded. Rubrics should be given to students at the same time as the assignment so they will understand exactly what is expected of them. Rubrics should drive instruction. They should be the foundation upon which every assignment is created and of which all corresponding instruction is an extension. Rubrics help to focus the learning process regardless of the task or class or content. They offer structure and help maintain focus. In addition, when students know what is expected of them from the beginning, then it is much easier to hold them accountable while encouraging them to give their best. (2)

Rubrics can do something grades alone have never accomplished: They can define quality. They give students the criteria and terminology to respond to their own and others' work. How often have we heard students tell peers, "Oh, this is good," or "It's okay," because they aren't sure what specifics to address. During self- and peer-assessment, rubrics act as a guide so students can be specific about a piece of work. With rubrics, students can use the criteria to point to strengths and recognize specific needs of their own and their peers' papers or projects.

Rubrics also reduce the amount of time teachers need to grade or evaluate student work, helping monitor student performance throughout the process, identifying areas of need and support before the product is complete. Not only does the rubric provide in-depth feedback, it enables the teacher to give such feedback in a concise and clear manner, checking, circling, or highlighting parts of the criteria or the quality scale. However, rubrics are not really time-saving devices because time must be spent establishing the rubric (or explaining it to students, whether it is a teacher-, department-, or district-created rubric). When it comes to the final evaluation, however, a rubric that has been used for self- and peer-assessment will be clear to all involved and require little explanation. "The parameters have been set and [evaluation] becomes merely part of the process rather than an overwhelming hurdle" (St. Michel 1997, 3).

As we began to use rubrics in our own teaching, we found that the criteria were much easier to establish than the explanation or articulation of the quality. For example, a few semesters ago, one of the assignments in Kathleen's class asked pairs of students to demonstrate how they might use language across the curriculum to study a topic or theme, what Weaver (1994) calls a thematic framework. The students in the class developed an extensive rubric addressing what they felt was important for this framework (see Figure 3.4). The students listed under each category the components that they felt should be reflected in the framework and how that category could be demonstrated. For example, under Resources, which was category six, the students felt that competence in that area could be demonstrated by determining whether the resources:

- were appropriate to the theme,
- included both nonfiction and fiction,
- were adequate in number to provide choice, and
- included multimedia.

Figure 3.4   Thematic Framework Rubric

Thematic Framework: Criteria for Evaluation

	Much	Some	None
1. Web			
• Connections between/among categories			
• Categories relate to theme			
• Variety of subjects			
2. Transactional Objectives			
• Stated in transactional terms			

	Much	Some	None

- Goals, not activities
- Objectives appropriate to theme

3. Activities Appropriate to Objectives
- Meaningful activities
- Activities relate to objectives
- Activities relate to theme

4. Schedule
- Blocks of time/flexibility
- Daily reading/writing
- Minilessons/conference time

5. Reading & Writing Across the Curriculum
- Writing to learn through research
- Journals and/or logs
- Reading and writing in content areas

6. Resources
- Appropriate to theme
- Include fiction and nonfiction
- Adequate for activities, choice
- Multimedia

7. Teacher as Facilitator
- Student choice
- Cooperative learning
- Conferencing (tch/stu; stu/stu)
- Inquiry-based learning

8. Student-centeredness
- Choice
- Minilessons
- Student-needs driving instruction
- Centers/environment

9. Culminating Activity
- Appropriate and meaningful
- Puts closure on framework
- Students share with parents, etc.

10. Presentation
- Organized
- Neat
- Bibliography

The listing of criteria was clear to the students and seemed to describe adequately "what counted" or what should be in evidence somewhere in the project, but it was open enough to provide for individual ideas and creativity.

The articulation of quality was where they began to have difficulty. Three columns measured the *amount* of evidence by the terms *much, some,* or *none*. What was missing were gradations of quality that could not be measured by the existing rubric (at least not as clearly as hoped). What was needed was a better explanation of what made each criterion clear, perhaps using the students' explanations of the criteria as part of the articulation of quality.

We're not alone when it comes to having difficulty with quality gradations. Teachers and students succeed in listing criteria, but the gradations of quality remain vague, often falling back on traditional explanations such as "excellent" and "good" and using terms that don't define the quality of the work. For example, in Figure 3.5, Sheryl Mondock (1997) has defined the criteria for portfolios through the following: pride and effort, improvement of reading and writing skills, reflection, and completeness. However, the gradations of quality are *excellent, above average, much, average,* and *minimum,* a five-point rating scale. What determines if something is *excellent* or simply *above average?* Is it displaying *much* effort over *average* effort? How are these terms explained?

Figure 3.5   Portfolio Rubric

Rating of 5
- Excellent pride and effort
- Excellent improvement of reading and writing skills
- Excellent reflection for self-evaluation
- Portfolio complete: proof of supporting evidence

Rating of 4
- Above average pride and effort
- Above average improvement of reading and writing skills

- Above average reflection for self-evaluation
- Portfolio complete: proof of supporting evidence

Rating of 3
- Much pride and effort
- Much improvement of reading and writing skills
- Much reflection for self-evaluation
- Portfolio complete: proof of supporting evidence

Rating of 2
- Average pride and effort
- Average improvement of reading and writing skills
- Average reflection for self-evaluation
- Portfolio complete: proof of supporting evidence

Rating of 1
- Minimum pride and effort
- Minimum improvement of reading and writing skills
- Minimum reflection for self-evaluation
- Portfolio complete: proof of supporting evidence

No One Said This Was Easy: The Case for Validity

Many rubrics we use are invalid because we don't score what's important in the real-world application of the content being assessed. Instead we design rubrics to assess what's easiest to describe rather than what really matters. For example, most scoring rubrics in writing, both teacher generated and those published by testing companies, still look at the *parts* of writing rather than the writing itself. Although we profess to believe in a whole-to-part philosophy of learning with such parts taught as skills in context, we still tend to assess the skills or parts at the expense of the whole. We still try to quantify when we assess.

Let's look at one rubric, the Pennsylvania Writing Assessment Holistic Scoring Guide, used in secondary classrooms throughout the state (Figure 3.6). This rubric, like so many others, often becomes a model for classroom teachers as they devise their own rubrics to use in their classrooms. The descriptors for a top score of 6 include "sharp, distinct focus; sophisticated ideas that are particularly well developed; controlled and/or subtle organization; voice apparent in tone, sentence structure, and word choice; few mechanical and usage errors."

Looking at a rubric such as this, we can't help asking ourselves, "What does this teach students about writing?" More to the point, "What is the message about the purpose and definition of writing?" If writing is about communication and meaning-making and good writing relies on imagination, style, and voice, where are we assessing the *effectiveness* of writing rather than the *correctness* of writing? Although parts are important to effectiveness and should be addressed, the effects of the piece as a message or discourse should also be assessed if the writer is to get feedback that is similar to the response of a reader. Bob Dandoy (1996), a teacher at Karns City High School in Pennsylvania, once conferenced with a student who wrote a piece about her dad and what he meant to her. The emotions she felt were revealed through a series of prose snapshots of her dad, watching him work around the house, vacations shared, private personal moments. As Bob read the piece, tears began to well in his eyes. He was thinking of his own daughter. He told his student there were a few details to clean up, but in general it was ready for the "real test." Bob offered to show her some fancy fonts on the computer if she'd like to give it to her dad for Christmas. She said, "No. His birthday's in November—that's when I want to give it to him." She printed out a good copy, wrapped it up in a box, and took it home. Bob later asked the student what her dad thought of the writing. The student said, "He cried." Bob told us he couldn't think of a more authentic assessment than that.

Although the rubric from the state mentions content, it uses vague terms such as *substantial, specific,* and *illustrative* as

Pennsylvania Writing Assessment Holistic Scoring Guide

6	5	4	3	2	1
• sharp, distinct focus	• clear focus	• adequate focus	• vague focus	• confused focus	• absence of focus
• substantial, specific, and/or illustrative content; sophisticated ideas that are particularly well developed	• specific and illustrative content	• sufficient content	• content limited to a listing, repetition, or mere sequence of ideas	• superficial content	• absence of relevant content
• obviously controlled and/or subtle organization	• logical and appropriate organization	• appropriate organization	• inconsistent organization	• confused organization	• absence of organization
• writer's voice apparent in tone, sentence structure, and word choice	• precision and variety in sentence structure and word choice	• some precision and variety in sentence structure and word choice	• limited sentence variety and word choice	• lack of sentence and word choice variety	• no apparent control over sentence structure and word choice
• few mechanical and usage errors	• some mechanical and usage errors	• mechanical and usage errors not severe enough to interfere significantly with the writer's purpose	• repeated weaknesses in mechanics and usage	• mechanical and usage errors that seriously interfere with the writer's purpose	• mechanical and usage errors so severe that writer's ideas are difficult if not impossible to understand

NON-SCOREABLE (NS)

- Is illegible; i.e., includes so many undecipherable words that no sense can be made of the response
  or
- Is incoherent; i.e., words are legible but syntax is so garbled that response makes no sense
  or
- Is a blank paper

OFF-PROMPT (OP)

- Is readable but did not respond to the prompt

CHARACTERISTICS OF EFFECTIVE WRITING

FOCUS	CONTENT	ORGANIZATION	STYLE	CONVENTIONS
• demonstrates an awareness of audience and task	• Information and details are specific to topic	• logical order or sequence is maintained	• precise language	• mechanics: spelling, capitalization, punctuation
• establishes and maintains a clear purpose	• Information and details are relevant to focus	• paragraphs deal with one subject	• effective word choice	• usage (e.g., pronoun references, subject-verb agreement)
• sustains a single point of view	• Ideas are fully developed	• logical transitions are made within sentences and between paragraphs	• voice, tone, originality of language	• sentence completeness
• exhibits clarity of ideas		• Introduction and conclusion are evident	• variety of sentence structures, types, and lengths	

the content descriptors. Terms such as these may be operationally defined by the use of anchor papers when training holistic scorers, but these do not help a writer. A writer who is told to write "sophisticated ideas that are particularly well developed" would probably feel this advice is in the same category as the parental advice given upon leaving for the evening: "Drive carefully." Our son Jason would look at us and say, "Gee, I planned on driving inattentively and with reckless abandon." The writer might say, "Thank goodness you told me; I was planning on writing superficial content (score #2) . . ." Allan Collins and Dieter Genter (1989) offer descriptors such as *clarity*, *persuasiveness*, *memorability*, and *enticingness*. However, it's important that the writers (and assessors) understand the meanings of such descriptors, perhaps through the use of models and anchor papers, as used during the process of holistic scoring. When using rubrics, scoring must be valid as well as reliable.

Although some publications have models of generic rubrics, teachers find that, along with their students, they have to create their own rubrics to reflect their curriculum, their students' interests and needs, and their own teaching style. What's exciting but also somewhat challenging about this type of assessment tool is that it empowers teachers and students; the decisions about what is important are not left up to a publishing or testing company. Teachers and learners take responsibility for understanding and establishing what is important.

When we teach the I-search research paper (Macrorie 1988), we share examples of various papers and we ask our students to comment on the strengths and weaknesses. These comments help construct the rubrics we use to guide the writing of and the evaluation of the papers. Heidi Goodrich (1996) believes that words like *good, satisfactory,* and *poor* need to be defined operationally and suggests that teachers share models of student work to define criteria through example. Students may recognize when a product is good, but they need to work at verbalizing what it is that makes that piece "good." If the purpose of a rubric is to teach as well as to evaluate, terms must be defined for students (and for teachers). If a teacher wants to stress creativity, the class might look at models of creative works and define the concept with concrete qualities of creative work. In addition to avoiding unclear language, rubrics should not use negative language.

Teachers need to look at what's important in the real-world application of what they are teaching and learn to make judgments about exemplary performance, not just what is easiest or least controversial. This isn't easy; it takes practice and a great deal of thought and discussion. Goodrich (1996) believes in listing specific criteria and articulating the descriptors for gradations of quality. Some find it easiest to begin with extreme nodes, the *excellent* and *poor* ends of the scale, and then work toward the middle. One caution would be to avoid a five-point scale that students mentally convert to the traditional A, B, C, D, and F grades. While Terrie St. Michel (1997) advises generating the rubric at the same time as the assignment, Grant Wiggins (1993) believes that not only must the scoring be done after the performance but the rubric should also be revised and made final after the performance is completed. To arrive at a final rubric, Goodrich suggests that teacher and students practice using the tentative rubric given with the assignment to see what might be unclear and what works. (This might be comparable to the process of using anchor papers to train scorers in holistic scoring.) Wiggins suggests that "the most valid design procedures involve working backward from the criterion performance and from concrete models of diverse levels of performance. What too few practitioners seem to understand is that scoring rubrics must be derived *after* we have a range of performances in hand, so as to ensure that our descriptors and discrimination procedures are not arbitrary" (211). This is why it is so important to involve students throughout the process and not to consider our tentative rubrics as final evaluation tools devised before the process and the product can evolve.

No One Said This Was Easy, But It Can Be Done

While Rick Chambers (1997) was teaching at Kitchner-Waterloo Collegiate and Vocational School, he negotiated with his class the assessment rubric for their action-research essay. Rick explains:

We did the usual Grant Wiggins-Smokey Daniels type of discussion about how a piece of writing like this should be evaluated: What are we looking for? What should it say? How should it be written? Because the topics for the action research were so diverse, the students thought that the essay assignments might be equally diverse. We talked about that for a while, but it became apparent that even though the topics might be diverse, the form probably wouldn't be. . . .

So, we did the assessment brainstorming, and put all of the students' suggestions on the blackboard. Then, I asked them to lump the individual points into larger categories, and we arrived at these four: style, structure, quality of argument, and presentation. And then, I told them that they had 100 points to distribute among the four categories [see Figure 3.7]. We argued about that for a while, and eventually reached consensus (more or less) on this arrangement: 20, 20, 50, and 10, respectively. It's always interesting listening to the students' arguments about how to do this: The reasoning here was that the essay was content driven, according to the kids, so most of the marks should be for content. I didn't really agree with that: I wanted the reflection, and therefore possibly the structure, to be worth more, but I lost. The whole exercise was quite democratic, especially for a school setting, and I didn't want to impose my values on their opinions. As well, this was not the first time that we had done this kind of negotiated assessment thing during the semester, and so the students knew how to play the game.

After we had agreed on the mark values for each category, I then asked what one would have to do to earn 20/20 in the "style" category, or in the "structure" category, or 50/50 in the "quality of argument" category, or 10/10 in the "presentation" category. More discussion. I continued to write the students'

86

Figure 3.7 Writing Evaluation Form

Student Name: _____

STYLE: Mechanical Accuracy, Grammar, Spelling

20- - - - - - - - - - - - - - 16 - - - - - - - - - - - - - - - - 12 - - - - - - - - - 8 - - - - - - - - 4 - - - 2

Mechanical accuracy; complete sentences throughout (dialogue excepted); punctuation used correctly; sentence structure accurate; no major errors; diction appropriate; usage correct	One or two major grammar errors; spelling errors; meaning unimpaired	Several major grammar errors; awkward constructions; spelling errors; communication of ideas impeded

STRUCTURE: Organization of Material; Consistency; Logic

20- - - - - - - - - - - - - - 16 - - - - - - - - - - - - - - - - 12 - - - - - - - - - 8 - - - - - - - - 4 - - - 2

Well organized; recognizable form; on topic; consistent tone; clear beginning, middle, end; paragraphs intact; coherent; smooth and flowing; identifiable thesis; strong transitions; forceful, memorable introduction and conclusion; audience addressed	Focus generally clear with logical organization; paragraphs generally developed, focused; a few abrupt transitions; introduction and conclusion need work	Focus somewhat unclear; weak organization; topic sentences not related to thesis; some abrupt transitions	Blurred focus

QUALITY OF ARGUMENT: Information; Argument; Believability

50 - - - 45 - - - - 40 - - - - 35 - - - - 30 - - - - 25 - - - - 20 - - - - 15- - - - 10 - - - - 5- - - - 0

Memorable, persuasive, clear, enticing; fascinating; good information; ideas are credible and verifiable; clear thesis, convincing argument; questions are answered; degree of difficulty is appropriate	Good information and ideas; competent development of argument and information; indications of thought and reflection; adequate evidence; little originality	Overly simple thesis; insufficient development of ideas; weak textual evidence	No clear thesis; lack of depth in development or elaboration of ideas; little textual evidence

87

PRESENTATION: Legibility; Appearance; Process Components
10 - - - - - - - - - 8 - - - - - - - - - - 6 - - - - - - - - - - 4 - - - - - - - - - - 2 - - - - - - - - - 0

Word processed, punctual; title page; Writing Center slip; neat; double spaced; essay title is relevant	Word processed; punctual; Writing Center slip; neat	Word processed; incomplete without Writing Center slip

ADDITIONAL COMMENTS:

TOTAL: _____

criteria and suggestions on the blackboard, and had a student recorder in the class taking notes for me as well, so that I wouldn't have to recopy everything when the class was over. Predictably, some of the areas took longer to decide upon than others. For instance, the students, even at this late stage of their high school careers, were unclear about what would constitute a perfect mark in the "style" area. So, we spent some time talking about that. What that did, as well, was promote a greater interest for individual students to make sure that their essays were well crafted, coherent, organized, and interesting. It led to a lot of [opportunities for teaching and] one-on-one coaching for me, but it was worth it because the students knew from the outset what was expected of them, because they had helped to establish the criteria. (1–2)

Neil Cosgrove, an English teacher at Slippery Rock University, involves his students in developing the criteria used in his rubrics in his college writing classes. Neil asks his students to bring to class samples from their own writing or someone else's writing, including published writing, that they consider *good*. The samples the students bring are taken from a variety of sources: traditional classics ("The Tell-Tale Heart" by Edgar Allan Poe and *The Grapes of Wrath* by John Steinbeck); newspaper stories; advertising copy (the ad for a new Chevy Lumina); popular writers (from Dean Koontz to Maya Angelou); famous speeches (Martin Luther King, Jr.'s "I Have a Dream");

less well-known works ("Body Ritual Among and Nacirema" by Horace Miner, *The Ruby Knight: Book Two of the Elenium* by David Eddings, *Emigre #25* by Erik van Blokand, *A Distant Mirror: The Calamitous 14th Century* by Barbara Tuchman, and "Manzanar, U.S.A." by Jeanne Wakatuski Houston).

In class, Neil's students work collaboratively in groups to try to articulate what traits made each piece of writing "good." Neil then collects the individual groups' contributions, copies them, and distributes them to the class. Once more in groups, the students construct a description of the traits of good writing. Neil considers this an inductive rubric because the students work from the specific instances of good writing to the general categories. Neil's inductive rubric becomes the guidelines for his writers and the evaluation checklist used for the grading of their papers (see Figure 3.8).

Figure 3.8   Inductive Rubric

Characteristics of an "A" Paper:
- The focus of the paper remains clear throughout; moreover, the writer maintains a consistent tone or "voice."
- The writer uses ample details, examples, or other kinds of supporting information that make the paper's ideas persuasive while holding the reader's interest.
- The paper's ideas are connected in a way that makes sense to the reader; paragraphs flow smoothly into each other, in part because clear transitions are employed.
- The style fits the purposes and audiences for the paper, with appropriate word choices and carefully constructed sentences.
- The writer demonstrates a knowledge of standard usage and of the conventions for punctuation and spelling, and employs that knowledge to serve the purposes of the paper.

Characteristics of a "B" Paper:
- The writer maintains a consistent tone; some of the reasons for writing are momentarily lost.
- The writing holds interest, but supporting information is somewhat less ample, less relevant, and, therefore, less persuasive.
- The reader can easily follow the logic that holds the material

together; nevertheless, the organization may be commonplace, and it does not propel the reader forward in a seemingly inevitable direction.

- Sentences are structured in a clear but also predictable manner; word choices may be repetitive or not quite the right fit for the purposes or audiences.
- There are a few inadvertent deviations from standard usage or punctuation and spelling conventions, but none that seriously distract the reader from the content.

Characteristics of a "C" Paper:
- The writer loses track of his overall intent and/or his "voice" on occasion.
- Some ideas are supported by adequate examples or other kinds of detail; others are not, and the writer seems unconcerned that the reader will be dissatisfied.
- The governing trait is inconsistency; some ideas are clearly connected, others might be if transitions were employed, while still others may seem "tossed in" to "flesh out" the paper.
- Sentences may be awkwardly or confusingly structured; word choice is characterized by repetitiveness and/or imprecision; clarity has become more of a concern than appropriateness.
- Deviations from standard usage and/or punctuation and spelling conventions are commonplace; a few may distract the reader from the meaning the writing seeks to convey.

Characteristics of a "D" Paper:
- The paper lacks any kind of "hook"—a clear set of purposes or an identifiable personality or voice.
- There are few supporting details or examples that will serve to make the writer's assertions believable.
- An organizational scheme is not discernible; ideas are tossed on the page in no apparent order, often in one long paragraph.
- The meaning of some sentences is lost, perhaps because of poor grammar or excess verbiage; the writer is struggling to discover meaning, rather than to communicate meaning to a reader.
- Deviations from common usage and accepted conventions are so frequent they are annoying; a reader may be tempted to give up wading through them all.

Neil develops a different checklist for each class, using his students' actual words and expressions. Neil believes this does two things: It helps students develop a vocabulary for talking about writing and traits of good writing and it puts them in the evaluation process. His students not only learn in the act of wrestling with the discovery of what "good" writing is, but they know that the grade they receive may be subjective, but not arbitrary (Strickland and Strickland 1997).

Neil Cosgrove would agree with Rick Chambers' comments:

> As Grant Wiggins and others have urged, assessment (sitting beside) is an ongoing element of the curriculum, and not something that happens at the end of a unit. A writers' workshop class is the perfect example of an assessment situation. Development of rubrics with student input and design creates an egalitarian, democratic environment where everyone knows the criteria for success, and can try to achieve them. Cooperative creation of the descriptors for the rubric ensures that everyone in the class knows what and how to achieve; peer assessment, using the rubric, leads to self-assessment and adjustment, and those changes usually lead to improvement. (Chambers 1996, 13–14)

> Interestingly, the marks for the essays were quite good in the last analysis because the students knew what to expect, had been part of the process of establishing criteria, and had the rubric in front of them the whole time that they were writing the essay (or, at least they could have had it in front of them if they had chosen to). As I said, however, we had used this same approach to writing and speaking assignments all semester, and so the process was not new, and student familiarity with it certainly helped them on this last major assignment. Ultimately, of course, because the students are part of the assessment process—both in helping to establish the criteria and then performing to meet those criteria—their marks are better: What a surprise! (Chambers 1997, 2)

It is important to remember that creating practical, useful rubrics takes time. Rubrics should be employed as often as possible for self- and peer-assessment during the process. The same rubric can be used for both assessment and evaluation purposes. The rubrics themselves may need revision during the process, and Heidi Goodrich (1996) cautions that when rubrics are revised, students should be clear about the revisions themselves and the need for such revisions. Although the final grading or evaluation may go quickly, class time is needed for the development and use of such assessment tools as rubrics. However, the process of assessment itself is a part of the learning process and is worth class time if the teacher understands the value of students' involvement in the process.

Thoughts for Further Inquiry

1. Discuss some examples of performance assessments you've seen or used. Were these authentic? Why? If not, how could they have been designed to be authentic assessments?
2. Discuss examples of alternative, authentic, and performance assessments. Can you think of ways assessments can be all three?
3. Look at a test you have constructed or one you have taken. Decide if it is a one-story (gathering), two-story (processing), or three-story (applying) test. If it's a *lower* story test, how could it be rewritten to give students a chance to apply what they've learned?
4. In a group, design a rubric. Decide on criteria and gradations of quality. Realizing that this rubric would evolve as you and your students use it, how would you ensure that all descriptors were clear?
5. Look at a rubric you've used as a teacher or as a student. What are its strengths? How could it be revised to become more informative?

4

Portfolios

I have heard people say, "The difference between a portfolio and a folder of student work is purpose." I would go further and say, "The difference between assessment that is busywork and assessment that reflects the essence of our teaching is what we and our students make of what we collect."

—Lucy Calkins

"We're often unsure whether . . . students have actually learned the skills or the knowledge, or whether they're going through the motions, only to forget everything later," says Rick Chambers (1996), a former secondary teacher in Ontario, Canada. So Rick decided why not "ask the students how they're doing? . . . Ask them to monitor their own progress, and get them to tell us how they're doing?" Rick found portfolios "a natural way for students and teachers to track the learning experience over a period of time" (1).

Portfolios are nothing new. Stockbrokers speak of a collection of investments as portfolios. Jim's sister Melissa takes a portfolio of her previous advertising campaigns when she calls on potential new clients. Artists and architects have traditionally used portfolios to showcase their work, demonstrating who they are, what their strengths are, and the range of their ability. Portfolios in education refer to any collection of work that *showcases* the student as learner, from writing folders to scrapbooks to mandated collections of work. The notion of using portfolios in schools grew out of a concern for assessing performance over time. What should be in portfolios? Sometimes students are allowed to select what is included in a portfolio; unfortunately, the selection is controlled more often by teachers and school districts. Who should decide what is included in portfolios? Portfolios can be used for assessment, for evaluation, as permanent records of student achievement, for teaching, for grading, for celebrating, or just for collecting. How should portfolios be used?

There are no formulas for using portfolios; however, as with any new strategy or technique in teaching, *how* it's done grows out of an understanding of *why* it's done. With this in mind, teachers learn to use portfolios through their students' as well as their own personal experience with portfolios. We can't profess or claim that we have answers to all the questions concerning portfolios; like other ideas, this one grows and changes as teachers and students discover together how portfolios can best be used in different situations and in different communities of learners. Instead, we'll discuss *possibilities* for portfolios—possibilities that grow out of a belief in student decision making and a hope that techniques we use in the classroom are authentic and meaningful to the learner.

Bonita Wilcox (1996), a teacher at Duquesne University, suggests creating a teacher's portfolio as a self-evaluation tool and as a way for teachers to present themselves—a professional portfolio. A teacher's portfolio can be as formal as a collection of documents related to a job application, but it need not be any more formal than a collection of writings in process, collections of book reviews to remind one what to read next, a photocopy of a current/favorite article, samples of lesson plans, etc. We would encourage all teachers, whatever the content area, to create their own portfolio as they help students create theirs. This might be difficult for some, and the most common excuse we hear is a lack of time; however, if teachers are reading, writing, and learning with their students, they can use a portfolio to self-evaluate and set goals for themselves and their classroom. The teacher's portfolio may be a content portfolio as is the case with a writing portfolio, it may be a professional portfolio (such as

Bonita Wilcox suggests), or an assessment portfolio. Once again, the only "rule" is that whatever is collected and presented is useful, reflective, and designed to help one grow.

Ownership/Managing Portfolios

"Students own the portfolios," says Jane Blystone (1997b), of North East High School. Work in a portfolio rightfully belongs to the student who created it, and thus, teachers should show respect for the student's property (Tierney, Carter, and Desai 1991). Jane explains that she feels a portfolio is "a kid's brain on paper. I can only look and help the student to plan strategies for writing growth, but I can't own their minds or their portfolios" (4).

Jane has found that her definition of portfolios has grown each time she approaches the process with a new class. Jane explains,

> Perhaps that's because I look at portfolios as a work of art—each one new and unique to the owner. I do not feel students should be thought of as products of a school system. Rather, they're works of art in progress, growing and changing as they absorb and integrate knowledge from school and their cultures into their lives. This is something we don't do often enough in classrooms because we want all our students' papers to look alike and all students to have the same knowledge when they leave us. Maybe that is why we love Scantron machines and number two pencils. Many educators assume that students are learning if they fill in bubble sheets correctly, or do matching questions with expertise, or are eager every day in class to answer what I call low yield questions, like "Who is the president of the United States?"

Jane continues,

> Some educators spend precious moments in the faculty room complaining about how students can never transfer knowledge ("facts") to real world situations. I say they are absolutely right

but only because students have never been permitted to own what they learn. When the teacher determines what the child has "learned," calling it right or wrong, no workplace thought processes operate. Workplace thinking requires evaluation, planning, organizing, working in teams, negotiating, and reworking ideas, but students are rarely allowed to do that in school. So how do we think students can connect learning with real life when real life operates differently than our school environment? This is why it is so important for students to own portfolios. (4–5)

Purpose for Portfolios

Teachers should discuss with students how and why the portfolios are being used, what criteria might be used when selecting pieces for their portfolio, and how such choices might demonstrate their strengths, interests, effort, and development in the content area (Tierney, Carter, and Desai 1991).

Rick Chambers (1996) says that he wanted to use portfolios as "a method of letting students choose their best work for evaluation, to see what criteria they used when deciding what was best, to find out what they perceived as essential learning in the course, and to discover what else they wanted or needed to learn. . . . This act of asking students to talk about their learning is a humbling experience for both the student and the teacher. The student takes inventory of his/her learning so far, and honestly has to tally up his successes and failures. The teacher can see where more work needs to be done on his/her part in presenting skills or knowledge or adjusting strategies to help the student achieve" (1).

There are teachers whose students have taught them about the possibilities of portfolios. Rick is one of those teachers. "Predictably, when one asks students to be honest in an assessment of their learning, the course content, the strategies used in the presentation of ideas, and where the course and the students' learning should go next, the results are revealing, candid, and mostly, refreshing" (1–2).

Ongoing and Updated

Jane Blystone says that her students know that they are responsible for their portfolios because the portfolios belong to them, not to Jane, the district, or the state. They keep their working pieces in a big box in the computer lab rather than in Jane's room. Jane explains, "Most tend to leave them in the box in the lab, so they don't forget them or lose some of the materials they are working on at any given moment." They can update their portfolios, "taking anything out and adding anything that they'd like to include from any writing that they've done in or out of class. Some keep poems that they have written from past years as well as songs, drawings, etc. The Big Box is like a safe house, a place from which special things will be gleaned at a later date" (1997b, 2). Portfolios should be thought of as developmental, allowing students to make constant updates to document their progress (Tierney, Carter, and Desai 1991). For this reason, earlier pieces are often not removed. How frequently portfolios are updated and the number of pieces they contain depends on the length of the course and purpose for the portfolio.

Tierney, Carter, and Desai (1991) suggest that portfolios be thought of as vehicles for ongoing assessment by students rather than as static objects. Portfolios represent active processes ("selecting, comparing, self-evaluation, sharing, goal-setting") more than products. One student, Melanie Rahn, appreciates the *selecting* activity: "Another thing I have learned about myself is that if I don't like the topic I am writing about after the first three paragraphs, then I may as well start over. In the past I have tried to keep writing things I wasn't too happy with, and all it did was make me frustrated and upset, and when I get like that there is no hope of writing anything half decent. It is better for me to just cut it off early, and think of something else" (Chambers 1996, 12).

Another student, Sarah Smith, concurs, "Although it's important to know what needs to be improved when evaluating yourself, it's also good to know what your strengths are. Then, you can build on those strengths and become an even better writer. I think that I am good at catching the reader's attention at the very beginning of my stories and essays. I like to write things that I would enjoy reading myself, and I try to keep that in mind whenever I write. I also think that I have improved at writing for a specific audience. For the contests we entered, we really had to think about who the judges were, so that the language we used was appropriate" (Chambers 1996, 12).

Jim Mahoney (1997), of Miller Place High School in New York, knows that "to assess their growth over a period of time, students need lots of opportunities to look back, before looking ahead to what's next for them." Jim calls this "the reflective stance." Jim's students learn to take a reflective stance when establishing goals for themselves for the next quarter.

> New York State has four standards for the language arts that ask students to acquire and use information, create and respond to texts, synthesize and analyze information, and use information for social interaction. Rather than have just the teacher be responsible for selecting activities in these standards, we ask students to decide what they can do in the standards and set attainable goals for themselves, goals which have results that can be measured in some way. This provides for a great deal of choice within the fields outlined, and it also produces a variety of products by the end of the year. It is no wonder students have lots of things that they want to include in their portfolios. In the course of a marking period, I ask my students to have six or seven finished pieces of writing. By the year's end, students have at least twenty pieces (some far more), so they still have some tough choices for fitting things in. (11–12)

Pro Choice

One of the most important elements in portfolio assessment, in fact, is student choice. Tierney, Carter, and Desai (1991) suggest teachers afford students choices to pursue their interests, to make decisions, to collaborate, and to collect samples of their work. Students need opportunities to analyze and compare their pieces and to conference with peers and the teacher about their decisions. Jane Blystone (1997b) lets her students pick the writings they wish to revise and says, "I give them total authority to change their minds and select another writing if that one doesn't seem to come together. I have even encouraged them to write a totally new piece if they can't seem to get any to work into a satisfying essay. I do not spend any time telling them the *form* for essays, as many English teachers do, choking them with the five-paragraph essay format." Jane says she simply tells them that "if they have something to say, then they should say it. I suggest several essay writers for them to read, such as Henry David Thoreau, who is in their literature textbook" (2).

One of Sarah Smith's final comments in her portfolio was this: "I am glad that, for once, we were given the opportunity to choose what we thought was our best writing. Usually, only the teacher's opinion counts and we tend to only look at the mark we received. This assignment allowed us to learn about ourselves, and decide what meant the most to us" (Chambers 1996, 8). Rick Chambers says, "Even though the idea of choice has always been a staple of writing classes and assignments, I had never realized how important this element was for students until the portfolio comments came rolling in" (8). Another of his students, Heidi Braun, agrees: "There are no restrictions placed upon me when I'm writing a journal entry and this is a type of writing that I enjoy as a result of this freedom. Each week when I sit down to write, I get excited knowing that I can fill the pages with whatever I choose. A journal entry allows me to experiment with style, topic, tone, and length" (10). Although Rick's "students' journal entries were often very personal, [they] were also sometimes literary and reflective. Essay contest entries, poems, descriptive passages, responses to literature in this or other courses all formed part of the body of work from which students could choose. . . . Being able to articulate what is good about their writing is part of their self-assessment, and also clearly reflects what they have learned. The reflective conclusion of the portfolio where students talk about what they have learned is another important element of the assignment" (9–14). In her reflective conclusion to her portfolio, one student, Louise Jessup, realized how important her work as tutor was to her growth as a writer herself: "Being a Writing Center tutor has allowed me to realize places where my writing needs improvement and . . . I can state, with all confidence, that I am a better writer because of my role as a tutor. [Peer conferencing with] others has enabled me to better edit my own work, allowing me to produce polished and confident pieces of writing" (5).

"If learning is to be a lifelong process," Rick concludes, "then students have to understand how they learn, and how they can improve, and what they should learn next. Continuous improvement and lifelong learning are the primary outcomes of this assignment" (14).

Teachers' Roles
in the Portfolio Classroom

In a classroom where portfolios are used for assessment and evaluation, the teacher's role is varied and often difficult. There is a fine line between control and support; between choice and lack of guidance. Tierney, Carter, and Desai (1991) suggest that teachers should explain to students what the teacher's role will be in selecting work for student portfolios: helping students articulate reasons for including each piece in their portfolios and encouraging students to be explicit as to why they feel certain pieces should be included and how they reached their decision. "The portfolio's element of choice, as noted above, is a crucial part of the assignment. Students need to have the freedom to make choices about what they think is their best writing, and then to defend those selections in their introduction," says Rick Chambers (14). Teachers must find their role so students can learn to be responsible for their own learning. Jane Blystone (1997b) has found ways to support her students in her classes while providing them with the opportunities to learn to make important choices; however, these choices must be based on criteria that it is often the teacher's responsibility to help students discover. Jane explains, "I try to use conferencing to help them avoid being 'pack rats' with their work. We do oral negotiation to help them move through some pieces to make them presentable, or as some call them, final form. For example, we do four essays at the beginning of the trimester. I let them sit for three weeks unattended in the working portfolio. Then, the student has a conference with me and I ask nontypical teacher questions, such as, Which one did you like the most? Which was the easiest for you to write? Which do you think you could polish up if you were given time? Then, I suggest they revise the pieces that they selected to include in the showcase portfolio as they need a variety of writing styles in their final portfolio" (2).

Although the portfolios belong to the students in Jim Mahoney's (1997) classes, his role as teacher is one of facilitator, coach, supporter, and model. Jim explains, "Writing doesn't just come out of the sky for the portfolio. Students have to have been working all year. . . . Students work regularly in their writer's notebook, recording the wide-awake moments of their lives in as much detail as possible. They record their lives so that what seems quite ordinary today might prove very interesting in several weeks when it is reread or reshaped into a finished piece. In their writer's notebook, students must produce twenty pages of writing, the equivalent of two pages a week" (6).

Rick Chambers (1996) also believes the teacher's role is one of "coach, facilitator, listener, guide, and mentor. Periodically, [a teacher] breaks into a minilesson on a style or grammatical point. Most importantly though, he is part of the writing environment; he is writing when the students write, and he shares his problems and rough drafts with the students. He is learning with them, and modeling the process for them. The teacher shares his work in progress, and throws his rough drafts in with the students' for peer reading and assessment. He takes the same risks as he asks the students to take, and in so doing, demonstrates his vulnerability, which almost always forges an easy rapport with the class" (13).

Addressing Format Concerns

Tierney, Carter, and Desai (1991) suggest that teachers stipulate any formal considerations expected when beginning the portfolio process. For example, many teachers ask that portfolios include a table of contents, arranged by chronological order, by sections, or by themes. Some teachers, if they feel it's important to document growth, ask that all included work be dated. Other teachers ask that students write, on a separate sheet, the strengths that they feel each piece shows and why it was selected. Some teachers welcome the inclusion of peer responses to student work.

Kathy Simmons (1997), chair of the English department, says that students at Hempfield Area High School in Pennsylvania are required to maintain a writing folder throughout their four years of high school. Her directions to tenth-graders explain: "These folders will include writings . . . begun in the ninth grade . . . [and] done throughout each year—paragraphs, complete themes, rough drafts, revisions, essay responses—anything that constitutes discourse. Thus, the selections for the folder will include everything, at first. By the end of the year, both the student and the teacher will select several writings (at least five, including one per quarter to show development and improvement) to be placed in the folder and sent on to the next grade teacher. . . . At the end of the year, students will be able to remove any writings they wish, as long as several sample writings go on to the next teacher." Seniors at Hempfield also write a retrospective "Dear Reader" essay in addition to the work done throughout the year. In her letter, Carolyn Baker (1996) wrote, "During the past year, I learned how to really push myself. As I did in the past, I always gave my best effort, from the start. In the past, though, once I reached a certain level of quality in my work, I would sometimes stop. Now that I push myself further and harder, that early level (first plateau) will not suffice anymore. . . . Work that I used to consider my 'best,' I now consider not good enough, and I might work for hours or days to make it even better."

Jamie Sue Crouse (1996) spoke about a piece that she chose for her portfolio because of its personal significance: "My second favorite is . . . *One for Nine-One-One*. The paper does not rank among my best papers, but the message in it released a great burden and anger off my shoulders. Writing has always served as a vent for my energies, a release for my feelings. I highly recommend to everyone that they should read it. Though my statement sounds egotistical, my article contains the truth behind 9-1-1, a truth everyone should know and understand." Beth Spudy (1996) reviewed her strengths as a writer and then confronted what she calls her "one weak characteristic . . . wordiness. Since I type my rough drafts, I usually do not realize how many unnatural words I have added. One example of my wordiness appears in the second paragraph of the sample. . . . Through revision, I try to eliminate wordy sentences, but at times I add more words instead of deleting the unneeded words." Each student learns something about themselves and about the writing process in the process of reviewing the folder and writing the "Dear Reader" letter.

Jane Cowden (1996) requires her students at Big Spring High School in Pennsylvania to choose their three best works and include them in the portfolio with earlier drafts. Additionally, they are required to write three letters to their teacher (largely self-reflective), include a peer response for each selected writing, and check the format requirements (see Figure 4.1).

Figure 4.1 Portfolio Requirements

Portfolio #8　　　　　Name:_____
May 20, 1996

Three best works:
Title:_____ Early drafts:_____
Title:_____ Early drafts:_____
Title:_____ Early drafts:_____

Three letters to Mrs. Cowden: (check blanks)

_____ letters on reasons pieces were selected as best works, self-evaluation of your writing skills, how you did on reaching your writing goals this marking period (see your goal sheet)

_____ letter on self-evaluation of your reading, number of pages (on average) you read per week, how you did on reaching your reading goals this marking period (see your goal sheet)

_____ letter on books you have read this marking period, including titles and authors, plot summaries and evaluations (seniors only: Which of these books was/were written by an English or a non-American author?)

Three reader responses on your best works:

Reader Response 1 by _____

Reader Response 2 by _____

Reader Response 3 by _____

Checklist: (check blanks)

_____ Each best work must be typed or written in black or blue ink on white composition paper.

_____ All pieces must have your name, date and a MN (#).

_____ All letters must be in letter or memo form, including date, name of addressee, and name of writer.

_____ All letters must be typed or written in black or blue ink on white composition paper.

List titles of newly revised research paper(s):

Paper 1: _____

Paper 2 (seniors only): _____

Jim Mahoney's (1997) requirements for his students are similar; he asks that they include a table of contents, a reflection on themselves as writers, and how they used their writer's notebook. His students also reflect upon themselves as readers and how they used their literature logs. None of these activities are new for Jim's students because at the end of each marking period, he asks them to write a reflection on the work they have done in the previous ten weeks. The first time he asks his students to do this, Jim passes out a ditto that details reflective thinking called "A Backward Glance" (Figure 4.2). He asks them to review their writings to notice "patterns that begin to emerge. They also record how, when, where, and why they did their best and their worst reading and writing during the quarter. With these reflections recorded each marking period, they have ready access to how things were in the beginning of the year and can more easily write reflections for the whole year" (11).

Figure 4.2 A Backward Glance

Reflecting on the Writer's Notebook and Lit. Log after the quarter ends
This is not just an opinion. Give evidence from your notebooks.

Writer's Notebook
Take time to read over the entries in your writer's notebook and begin to notice the patterns that may begin to emerge. Consider some of the questions as you reflect.

- What is your strongest entry? Why? What importance does it have for you the person? For you the writer?
- What is the weakest entry or the one you're least interested in showing or even keeping?
- Where were you when you did most of your writing? Your best writing?
- Are you better off when a topic is given or put on the board or do you write best when you are alone and with your own thoughts and observations?
- What kind of growth have you seen on your writer's notebook? How important is this notebook to you?
- If a fire destroyed your things, how upset would you be if your notebook were lost? How useful has it become to you?
- Did you write anything this quarter because of something you read?

Literary Log
- What is your best lit. letter? How do you know? What do you use to rate it?
- Which letter would you like to show to a college recruiter? To your best friend?
- Which letter was your poorest? Why?
- What were the best responses you received from others? Why? Did anyone give you good feedback or make a good comment of recommendation to you?
- What were your best reading experiences? Why? How did you choose these books?

- What progress did you make regarding your lit. letters?
- How useful was your log? Would you be upset if you lost it in a fire?

Rick Chambers' (1996) portfolio description contains relatively simple formal requirements:

> The first portfolio, submitted in January, had to contain the four best pieces of writing that the student had done so far . . . selected from writings done in our course, and could include journal entries, formal essays, reflections, short stories, poems, or any other kind of writing. The students had to write an introduction to the portfolio indicating why these items had been selected as the best, and then write a conclusion to the portfolio in which the students would talk about what they had learned about writing, and themselves. The second portfolio in June would contain eight pieces of writing: they could include the four from January, or replace them with other works if they chose. The introduction and conclusion assignments remained the same. (3–4)

When we asked Jane Blystone (1997b) what is required in the portfolios, she explained,

> Students have three types of writing that they must include in their portfolio for a grade—essay, short story, and poetry. Their final essay is assessed—not graded—using the Pennsylvania Writing Assessment rubric [see Figure 3.6]. The short story is assessed using a rubric that I [adapted] from another source to match what students learn to do while writing a short story. . . . They also include a personal poetry anthology that they edit and compile from about twenty poems we write in class. The poetry anthology is assessed using a student designed rubric. Several years ago I asked students in the class to develop the assessment tool. It was so good that the kids now do not want it changed. When students get these three types of writings prepared for their showcase (graded) portfolio, I conference with them again and they write a self-assessment . . . and set some goals for them-

selves for future writing. . . . I want them to realize that writing is a lifelong experience. We look at each of the rubrics in their portfolio, discuss the contents, and use the rubrics as the basis for their grade (i.e., 6=A 5=B 4=C 3=D 2=F). (3)

Criteria-Based Evaluation

Teachers should evaluate portfolios based on criteria set up at the beginning of the process, criteria mutually decided upon by the students and by the teacher (Tierney, Carter, and Desai 1991). Peer evaluations, to be supportive and helpful, should be based on criteria that have been discussed.

Jane Cowden (1996) asks her Big Spring students to set reading and writing goals for themselves for each marking period (Figure 4.3) and then asks them to refer to these goals when self-evaluating their work in the portfolio (see Figure 4.1).

Figure 4.3 Reading and Writing Goals

By the end of this period, I, _____
                                    (print your name here)

plan to reach the following reading goals:
1.

2.

3.

I also plan to reach the following writing goals:
1.

2.

3.
Student's signature _____

Teacher's approval: (check one)
Approval as stated above: _____

Approval with adjustments: _____ (see below)
Adjustments:

Teacher's signature _____

As part of the assessment process, Jim Mahoney (1997) sets up the requirements for the portfolio, with student choice being central to the actual product, as he explained earlier. The portfolio process helps his students learn to reflect on what they have written or produced. In order to make good choices, however, the students need to learn how to self-evaluate. What makes a piece "good"? Jim has devised strategies to help students begin this reflective process.

> We ask students to select their five best pieces of writing but they must have some balance with prose and poetry. In some cases, we say that a literary analysis or some other whole class piece of a more scholarly nature must be included. The first question they ask is if they can put in more than just five pieces. "Absolutely! You can include whatever else you want, as long as you include those five pieces, the reflections on each of the five, and the other things required." Now the pressure is off because they can include some of the things they love which might not make the top five. Almost always, they will fill up every page available, generally forty-eight pages. (10)

Sharing and Celebrating Portfolios

Students need opportunities to appreciate each others' best work by sharing some pieces orally or through some other type of forum. Many teachers see the wisdom in sharing portfolios—with parents, other teachers, administrators, and other students (Tierney, Carter, and Desai 1991). Teachers should encourage students to share their work with their parents and help parents understand the value of a transactional approach to teaching and learning. Tangible evidence such as a portfolio will reassure parents that their children are learning everything prescribed by the curriculum and learning it in an atmosphere encouraging responsibility and goal setting.

Like the teachers at Hempfield Area High School, Jim Mahoney (1997) says, "We ask students to include a letter of introduction to their portfolio, a 'Dear Reader' letter. . . . In it, they ask for reader comments and they provide blank pages in the back of the book for that purpose. There are people who have helped them in one way or another, in their larger lives or with this portfolio . . . so we also suggest a dedication and/or foreword/acknowledgements page. . . . They also pore over the portfolios we have around from previous years. They study these things and begin to frame their own ideas" (10).

Rick Chambers (1996) believes, "the students-helping-students paradigm continues to be a marvelous learning tool." He quotes Tom Romano, "To be honest on paper is difficult and risky, quite an accomplishment in itself. To then share those true words with others is a profound act of faith and trust. Such writing and sharing requires a willingness to become vulnerable" (39). Rick says that "learning to give and take serious criticism about one's writing is a huge step for most of us: Writing is so personal that it takes a great leap in trust and faith to expose oneself to the comments of others. . . . As the course evolved, they learned to appreciate the comments of their peers" (7).

One of Rick's students, Becky Ayres, wrote: "When we write, we either read our work to three or four other [students] or share our ideas in a circle with the whole group. Constructive criticism is given and numerous suggestions are offered. This works extremely well, because again, as the group is small, it is a comfortable situation to express our ideas." Another student, Heidi Braun, concurred: "It is definitely an advantage for me to talk to others about ideas and to seek other opinions and suggestions" (8).

Teachers who use portfolios for assessment and evaluation soon discover that they must be shared, as all authentic showcase portfolios are, and students who produce their own portfolios are anxious and proud to share them with an audience. Such an audience, however, must be real. At our university, education majors must now compile a showcase portfolio before graduation, similar to Bonita Wilcox's professional portfolio, depicting in their own way who they are as teachers. As faculty, we help them set up criteria. They are then required to present these portfolios to an authentic audience—a panel consisting of two faculty members and two other stakeholders from outside of the university (school administrators, teachers, parents). Not only will these twenty-minute demonstrations provide a real audience for the students' portfolios, the actual demonstration will not be unlike a future interview for a teaching position. So that their portfolios are shared with peers, students present their portfolios in poster sessions, as we might at professional conferences. Sophomores and juniors are also welcome to attend these presentations so they can begin to think about their own portfolios.

Many teachers organize an in-school assembly or an evening social event as an opportunity for students to present their portfolios. In cases where such large events are impossible, resourceful teachers will organize in-class presentations of students' portfolios to others in the class, their teacher, and an outside guest, perhaps an administrator invited to attend the class. During these presentations, each student reads selections and reflects on his or her own learning, describing his or her development as a learner. Teachers who have tried these presentations report similar moments of success as students listen to each other share their portfolios.

Jim Mahoney found that part of the celebration was the look of the portfolio itself. The packaging and layout of the portfolio become extremely important to students—they're proud of the contents and they want the packaging to present their ideas well.

Jane Blystone (1997a) explains that a "coffee house" nighttime celebration she and her students held was actually the idea of one of her students, Emily. Having grown up in the 1960s, Jane was intrigued by the coffee house idea, so she asked Emily and a classmate to plan the evening.

They wanted to call it a "Celebration of Writing" and keep attendance exclusive. We made five invitations for each of the fifty-five students. The girls found two cappuccino/espresso machines and I brought a variety of teas from my cache. We set everything up in the cafeteria and students read poetry and shared their experiences of creative writing with the audience. At midpoint in the evening, we took a break from reading to allow parents and students to come over to the coffee/tea center and select their beverages. Once parents and teens had a beverage, they returned to their tables and had the opportunity to share portfolios with each other. Many lingered for some time and parents were thanking me for the opportunity to read their child's work and hear them read their work aloud. As in most schools, athletics takes a dominant position in our school, so some of my students rarely receive the kind of recognition that they experienced that evening. Their principal and other teachers took time out of a busy evening right before Thanksgiving break to celebrate the students' creativity. For most of the students in attendance that was great reward. I have started a new term with fifty new students and on the first day one of the students said, "Could we have one of those reading nights?" They were excited as they knew that only those with written invitations could attend. It is special, and yes, we are doing it again. (5–6)

Self-Evaluation of Instruction

As teachers review portfolios, in addition to evaluating student work, the collections provide answers as to whether and how well the objectives of the course have been met and what can be done in the future to support students further.

Part of Rick Chambers' purpose of his portfolio project was to assess where he was with his own teaching and learning process. Rick decided that "the aspects of writing that should be emphasized in schools are those that are most important: the pursuit of meaning and the development of each student's particular way of speaking with words on paper—voice. The whole area of metacognition, students realizing not just that they are learning, but how they are learning, is gratifying for both the student and the teacher. The student begins to recognize how he/she can turn learning into a lifelong activity, and the teacher can see how he/she can best help the student to achieve that outcome" (10). "The portfolio assignment was exciting, rewarding, and eventually fun for both the students and the teacher. . . . The next step for me is [self-evaluation]: What could work better? Which elements should be dropped, and which ones enhanced? As an exercise in the teacher's reflective practice, the portfolio project was a positive and energizing learning experience" (14–15).

Jim Mahoney (1997) says,

> Often, I take the portfolios, or at least some of them, home with me during the summer. I do this so that I can read them through from cover to cover, relishing every delicious part of the writing. Then I type a lengthy response about things I loved. I am specific about naming a poem or a reflection or a layout of a specific set of pages. One year, I wrote a separate individual poem to each student in response to the images I took away from their work. Last year, I found a professional poem or two and typed it next to my comments, connecting the poems with some of the same themes students had written about. While most students have not acknowledged with any great enthusiasm this particular aspect of my response, they will, I'm sure, someday look at this and read the poems I gave to them and understand even more. I will have touched them long after they had ever expected. (13–14)

Grading Portfolios

Most teachers who have worked with student-owned portfolios would rather not grade them, but the reality of it is, grades are so much of the secondary school culture that they are here to stay. If portfolios are to find a place in our classrooms, teachers must find ways to grade them and to report to parents, without turning these portfolios into competitive products or teacher-pleasing assignments. What about grading portfolios?

Maureen Neal (1997) says:

> When it's time to actually put a grade on portfolios, for example, I often cringe at what I perceive is the expectation that I should adhere to an implicit (almost ghostly) set of descriptors which represent my department's (unwritten) standard of acceptable writing quality. I find myself caught between my fear that I will be seen by my more conventional colleagues as a "soft" grader and my fear that I will be seen by my students as an untrustworthy, hypocritical demon who springs grading surprises on them after it is too late to do anything about it. I well remember one student . . . who came to me in tears after having received a B+ on her semester-end portfolio: "But I learned how to use a colon," she said, "And I never knew how to do that until now. Doesn't that count for anything?"
>
> In an attempt to counter these kinds of scenarios, I have tried Edward M. White's (1985) suggestion for a collaboratively constructed grading scale. Students contribute to it, I contribute to it, and we try it out on sample papers and then revise it through discussion and experimentation. Though this is helpful in many ways, it only seems to postpone the inevitably painful decision-making process, and it is not an acceptable solution to the conflict between process methodology and product-oriented assessment.
>
> The use of student-constructed grading scales in evaluating portfolios (the evaluation is done by the instructor) is . . . an attempt to extend the classroom climate created by interactive, transactional pedagogies to the assessment of the writing produced in those classrooms. Unfortunately, in my experience, the attempt to find an assessment tool which corresponds to a student-centered instructional style has not been successful. . . . Too often what happens is the abandonment of the student-constructed grading scales in favor of the instructor's own internal set of criteria about what constitutes good writing; that

judgment may be influenced by departmental expectations or an awareness of pressure for high standards, especially when a portfolio system is used. (2)

As we discussed in creating rubrics, Maureen Neal (1997) has found that

the descriptors generated by students are often ambiguous or contradictory, sometimes creating a confusing situation in which the characteristics for an A paper are less rigorous than those provided for a B paper. This situation can be remedied through discussion, but often the fact remains that there are no clear distinguishing lines between letter grade categories, even after discussion and revision.

Sometimes the problem was that we did not generate the grading scale early enough in the semester, so that there was too little time to "test" it by having students use it and modify it through trial and error. In addition, during the "testing" process, students seem to have inordinate difficulties in finding agreement about "grades" assigned to sample texts. Sometimes rationales given for grades (or numbers) assigned during the "testing" phase do not correspond to anything written on the grading scale.

Students often come to the conclusion that it is impossible to use the grading scale to evaluate their own work because the factors which contribute to a grading decision are, as they say, "infinite" and "unpredictable" and "you can't write down everything you use when you make up your mind." (2)

When we asked Jane Blystone (1997b) how she graded portfolios, she explained,

When I first started five years ago using "one grade for the portfolio" at the end of a grading period, I was taking a big risk because my school is very traditional, using percentages as the basis of the grading scale. I have never been sure what the difference between a 92 percent (B) on a piece of writing and a 93 percent (A) really meant. It did not tell me if a student could focus scattered ideas into an organized piece, or if the student could use a variety of strategies to formulate opinions, or use supporting details, or find a voice in a piece of writing, or spell correctly, or avoid dangling their participles, or splitting those ominous infinitives, etc. The first marking period I tried this, I had thirteen creative students in the class at the time, so we negotiated every detail. After each student had a culminating conference with me, I asked them to put the grade they thought they earned on a Post-it note and place it on the back of the portfolio. I read through the portfolios after class and, on a Post-it note on top of the portfolio, marked a grade that I thought they deserved based on the rubrics inside of the portfolio, my observations, their self-reflections, etc. When they came to class, I asked them to place their Post-it note beside mine on top to see how close we were. Ten of the thirteen had selected the same grade I had selected and two thought they deserved half a grade lower and one thought she deserved a half grade higher than I had given. They were thrilled that they [had a sense of] what good writing was and that they could come to the same conclusions as a teacher. (3–4)

Jim Mahoney (1997) has had similar experiences with the grading of portfolios. What he has found is that grades become secondary to the pride the student has for the portfolio itself; it showcases what the student can do and the students are proud of their accomplishment.

A student from a colleague's class was at work in the computer room one year, perfecting his portfolio to the very end. When the student showed his work to his teacher, he was so impressed that he asked if he could use it for a presentation he would be doing later that summer. The student agreed but added that the teacher couldn't have it until after the upcoming weekend. "It's graduation tomorrow," the student explained, "and all my relatives will be coming from all over, and my friends as well will be coming to my house after graduation. I want to be able to show this to everybody and let them see what I've created." (9)

Jim tells another story:

> It's the last day of school, 3:30. Grades have been turned in days ago. Most students are gone by 11:00, beginning their summer vacations, but I'm in the computer room with five or six students who still want to make their portfolios perfect. One ninth-grade student is still there with his father, who has come to help him do a few things to his portfolio, such as arranging the papers in plastic folders. They are late, expected home earlier, but still the father works away with his son, saying, "Mom is going to kill us," finally leaving at 3:45. Why would students stay after school is out, after their grades are already printed on the report cards? (8)

Jim believes it is because these portfolios have an authentic purpose.

Jane Blystone (1997a) has another perspective.

> I have a wide range of students from quick thinkers to those who are classified by my district as needing learning support teachers in mainstreamed classes. However, in my creative writing class all come in on the same level, no labels, even if they have taken this class before. This process has helped them to think and write beyond a level they even dreamed about. They have also learned to negotiate with others and focus on goals for future writing. They all engage in literacy. I don't worry about assessment anymore because these portfolios have come to prove their competence as writers better than any grade on any report card has ever shown. They have concrete proof that they can actually do something with the writing strategies they have learned and not just gather points for a grade. Isn't that the ultimate goal of education after all? (6)

After listening to teachers like Jane, Rick, and Jim, we're excited about the possibilities portfolios present to teachers, students, schools, and parents. However, not all schools are using portfolios in these ways. Maureen Neal (1998) says:

When I was a student teacher a little over twenty years ago . . .
portfolio evaluation was unheard of in public schools. When I gave
out my first set of grades, a student named Kevin was so upset by his
C that he spat on his report card in disgust—not once, but three
times. I've sometimes thought that the use of portfolio evaluation
would have soothed the wounds in that situation. However, I've
come to realize that, rather than solving most problems related to
grading, portfolio evaluation can create conflicts—both institutional and theoretical—much more disturbing and problematic
than those represented by a student spitting on a report card.
[Twenty years later I] found myself alarmed at the number of As
and Bs in my research writing course, which employed a portfolio
system of grading. As I figured grades, I scrounged to find someone
who legitimately deserved an F or a D (not many) or a C (a
few). . . . I believe portfolio evaluation is a good thing; so do count-
less others in the profession. Then why do I often feel uncertain
about grades in my portfolio-based writing courses?

    To be sure, in any kind of writing classroom, there is bound
to be some conflict, even anguish, over the assignment of grades
to student texts because issues of consistency, autonomy, role
relationships, and institutional politics that accompany our
evaluative behaviors. (1)

Maureen worries that the problems that attend the increasing
use of portfolio grading will be larger than the simple "expressions of reservation or caution associated with portfolios" and
she fears a "backlash, [that] if strong enough, could signal an
unwelcome return to traditional forms of grading" (2–3).

One problem specific to portfolio evaluation is that portfolios
are, by definition, a *collection* of work to showcase students as
learners in an organic process. Rubrics, which are often used to
evaluate portfolios, are designed for one specific assignment, as are
tests, to reveal a view of the learner at one frozen moment of time.

    The practice of using a static set of holistic descriptors to evalu-
ate a set of papers (rather than a single sample) is problematic not

only for students, but for instructors. Though Edward M. White (1985) believes that the process of evaluation used for single samples should be transferable to the assessment of portfolios, very little research has been conducted to determine whether or not this is a valid assumption, and students struggle with the same kinds of inconsistencies and questions about applying this process to portfolios that their instructors do. (Neal 1998, 2)

She continues,

At a recent national conference . . . a graduate teaching assistant admitted that the effort, energy, and rigid requirements for grading in his department's portfolio program had become so oppressive that it would be a relief to not have to work in a program which mandated portfolio assessment. This comment . . . made me aware that, for some instructors, the use of portfolios has become not a solution for instructional and assessment problems, but an unwelcome burden instead. In the same discussion . . . a woman who identified herself as a department chair expressed skepticism about the use of portfolios in individual writing classrooms because, as she explained, "The problem is the grades are so much higher with portfolios—all As and Bs." She attributed higher grades to the way that portfolio driven courses are taught. I had never before heard the concern for grade inflation linked so directly to portfolio-based pedagogy. (Neal 1998, 3)

And, Maureen asks,

What, exactly, is meant by the term "grade inflation"? I see grade inflation as an unwarranted preponderance of high(er) grades. Does portfolio grading contribute to that kind of grade inflation? To date, no empirical studies have been published which explore this crucial question, but the need for such research is imperative. . . . Jeffrey Sommers (1991), for example, notes that the possibility of grade inflation in a portfolio-driven course is an important concern, but he points out that "the [portfolio] system itself is designed to promote better writing by

118

the students, and it stands to reason that many students are going to be submitting portfolios that consist of writing better than they might be able to produce in a classroom employing a traditional grading system" (157). . . . Pedagogies that support a portfolio grading system (the emphasis on revision and response; student choice about what is to be evaluated in the portfolio; the opportunity for reflective commentary) contribute to an increased possibility for writing improvement, and therefore, higher grades are warranted for students who improve their writing. Is this a *problem?* (Neal 1998, 5–6)

Don't Kill a Good Idea

Donald Graves and Bonnie Sunstein (1992), in *Portfolio Portraits*, caution that "without careful exploration [of the uses of portfolios, their] use is doomed to failure. They will be too quickly tried, found wanting, and just as quickly abandoned" (1).

Maureen Neal (1998) agrees, "Certainly we want portfolio assessment to be reliable, consistent, and fair, but if the administrative task of creating reliability becomes more important and more overwhelming than the task of helping students learn to write, resistance—in the form of a desire to return to a more predictable, more quantifiable (but less direct) type of assessment—would not be surprising" (16).

To avoid repercussions and backsliding, Maureen offers three suggestions for protecting the proper use of portfolios. "First," she says, "it would be helpful for administrators to avoid . . . the mixed-use approach whereby portfolios produced in a classroom context for classroom purposes are also used by program administrators to test credibility or program validity. . . . We need to develop distinctions in the way portfolios are produced to satisfy different ends" (16–17). Portfolios often become the property of the district or state and students have little or no control over what is contained in them or how they are used.

Maureen's second suggestion is "if portfolio systems do employ outside evaluation, scoring criteria need to be designed and reviewed by all participants in a collaborative, egalitarian effort. Portfolio production and scoring should not be a top-down management decision; all participants need to be involved in decision-making if the aims of invested writing and consistency of evaluation are to be achieved" (17). When portfolios are used by a district or state as a large-scale assessment tool, the students often aren't even aware of the criteria that will be used to make judgments about their work. What is typical in many districts where portfolios are mandated is that a total control of the contents of the portfolio is determined outside the classroom. Teachers are given directions for portfolios in which the contents are completely specified from particular assignments to number and order of pieces to be included. Selection is often done by the teacher, based on the belief that students aren't capable of evaluating what is good work. We've also seen a tendency to standardize the instrument so comparisons can be made between students, schools, and groups.

Maureen's third suggestion is that "we may need to reconsider the very nature of reliability and how it can be achieved. . . . No one would argue that the entire notion of reliability should be tossed out the window, but rather that traditional concepts of reliability simply do not correspond well with the reading processes people use when they read (and evaluat) portfolios as writing products" (Neal 1998, 17).

Schoolwide Portfolios

One school district, North East High Schools, Pennsylvania, has undertaken a schoolwide cross-curricular portfolio project that seems aware of Maureen Neal's caution about the dangers of excluding students from the process. One of the teachers leading this project, Jane Blystone (1997c), was very concerned that the schoolwide portfolio would not be just another school mandate but would allow students and teachers to feel ownership of the process. Jane says, "Students do want to own their own learning, but they have not, until this portfolio project, been allowed to own it. Their ownership of the portfolios helped us move from a required graduation project to a portfolio that demonstrates growth over a long period of time" (1).

During the pilot project, ten teachers were trained in the process of portfolios, and they became mentors to 170 sophomores, the class of 1999. The description of the project that the students received is included as Figure 4.4. This year, the portfolio project included the ninth-graders, the class of 2000. At full implementation, every teacher in the high school will serve as a mentor to approximately ten students. Although the sophomores who piloted the program did not make a formal presentation of their portfolios last year, as seniors next year they will be asked to make a formal presentation of their portfolios. Each portfolio will be focused on an academic area of interest developed by the individual student. The guidelines for the Introduction and Self-Evaluation entries are included as Figure 4.5. Jane explains that the portfolios are used to assess students: "We are using the portfolios prepared last year to develop anchors for scoring like Pennsylvania Department of Education does with their writing assessment. However, we do not use the portfolios for a grade. Instead, the students will be held accountable for the culminating senior portfolio and an interview, both of which are required for graduation. At this point, we are in the midst of developing guidelines for the final project that the students must complete by their senior year. A tentative rubric has been completed (see Figure 4.6) and a purpose statement developed for the senior project" (2).

Figure 4.4 North East High School Cross-Curricular Portfolio Project

PURPOSE: To develop a broad picture of your academic growth over an extended period of time. The portfolio is not for a grade, but an assessment to help us get a better picture of what you can do with what you know as well as what you know.

TYPE: Cumulative, you will be putting the portfolio together between now and the middle of May. The portfolio will include examples of your best work over a period of time. Although you will be doing this with other students, your portfolio will be uniquely yours and will not look like anyone else's, so take great care in putting it together.

CONTENTS: Grade 10 will include works from English, science, math, social studies, and one other elective. Include one or two items from each of these areas during each of the three trimesters. You will also write an introduction, a table of contents, self-evaluation, and include entry slips with each entry. Your mentor will help you with the self-evaluation and entry slips as will your content area teachers.

MENTORS: Each sophomore has a mentor teacher who will help you prepare the portfolio, which will be scored in May. Your mentor will be in contact with you in the near future to help you get ready for this project.

Figure 4.5 Guidelines for Cross-Curricular Portfolios: Introduction and Self-Evaluation

Dear Student,
At this point in the portfolio assessment process, you will need to write an introduction and self-evaluation for the portfolio. Below are the instructions for these two pieces of writing. Be aware teachers other than your own will be scoring these portfolios, so the two pieces of writing need to be well written and neat. They must be on two separate sheets of paper as the introduction goes in the front of your portfolio and the self-evaluation goes in the back.

INTRODUCTION: Write a one page introduction telling who you are and some of the things you like to do (i.e., sports, a job, music, your pets, etc.) You need to also include some goals you have for yourself as a learner this year. Give the reader a glimpse of you as a person. You may include a picture of yourself in this section if you would like. Be sure there are no spelling or grammar problems that would hinder the reader's impression of you. Type the introduction, if at all possible. If not, please write it neatly in ink on composition paper available from your English teacher. Your teacher will advise you concerning the deadline for the final copy.

SELF-EVALUATION: This is a more technical piece of writing and can be more than but not less than one page. You need to evaluate each entry by comparing the two entries from each subject. You might use the following format for this piece of writing.

Paragraph 1 Write about yourself as a learner. How do you learn things? What are the easiest or most difficult things you have to do as a learner?

Paragraph 2 Write about the entries for English. What were the most difficult parts of each assignment? How did you improve as a learner over the course of the year in this class? Use examples from your entries to support your opinions.

Paragraph 3 Write about the entries for math. What were the most difficult parts of each assignment? How did you improve as a learner over the course of the year in this class? Use examples from your entries to support your opinions.

Paragraph 4 Write about the entries for science. What were the most difficult parts of each assignment? How did you improve as a learner over the course of second and third trimester in this class? Use examples from your entries to support your opinions.

Paragraph 5 Write about the entries for social studies. What were the most difficult parts of each assignment? How did you improve as a learner over the course of the year in this class? Use examples from your entries to support your opinions.

Paragraph 6 Write about your elective entries. What were the most difficult parts of each assignment? How did you improve as a learner over the course of the year in this/these class(es)? Use examples from your entries to support your opinions.

Paragraph 7 Write about any entries such as awards, recognitions you have received this year. This is an optional part of your portfolio.

Paragraph 8 Write several goals that you would like to accomplish in these core classes or other electives next year. Include how you have grown overall as a learner this year.

Jane feels that the most encouraging part of the project came when students evolved from being mere participants to becoming

Figure 4.6 North East High School Portfolio Rubric

Categories	Exemplary	Commendable	Adequate	In Progres
Focus	Purpose of individual portfolio extended. Entries connect to a central idea/ concept. Reflections are indepth and applicable in other areas.	Purpose of individual portfolio illustrated. Entries exceed requirements. Reflections are supported and validated by analysis.	Purpose of individual portfolio stated. Required entries present. Student reflects an understanding of acquired skills.	Purpose of ual portfol fused/no fc Entries mi Minimal o reflections
Organization	Cohesive plan. Creative.	Logical plan.	Attempted plan.	No plan.
Format	Pride in detail is apparent. No mechanical or usage errors.	Attention to detail. Minimal mechanical and usage errors.	Neat. Mechanics and usage errors do not interfere with overall presentation.	Sloppy. Mechanica usage error impede ov presentatic
Content	Quality pieces that demonstrate integration of skills: Communication Problem solving Life skills Technology Citizenship	Demonstrates improvement of skills: Communication Problem solving Life skills Technology Citizenship	Demonstrates a basic understanding of skills: Communication Problem solving Life skills Technology Citizenship	Lacks evid understanc skills: Communic Problem sc Life skills Technolog Citizenship
Interview	Presentation is carefully and purposefully developed with detail, reasons and facts. Good voice level, no hesitation, good eye contact.	Presentation is developed with details, reasons and facts. Planning is evident. Frequent eye contact; few nervous gestures or movements.	Information is adequate. Presentation shows evidence of some planning. Voice can be heard and understood. Occasional eye contact; some nervous gestures or movements.	Informatio inaccurate. Little evide planning. Awkward p Voice level low, distrac gestures.

team members in developing the design—asking probing questions from what the design of the entry slips (Figure 4.7) should be to what a good reflection might include. Student feedback and student reflection showed their teachers that students do want to learn and are very articulate about their own learning processes.

Figure 4.7 Example of an Entry Slip for Item Included in Portfolio

Portfolio Entry Slip

Name:_____ HR _____ Date _____

Subject:_____

Type of assignment: (lab. journal, simulation, research project, etc.)

What I learned from doing this assignment: _____

What I need to do to improve in this course: _____

Jane has high hopes for the future: "As these portfolios are emerging we see unique, quality portfolios that are not only connected to growth in content learning, but evidence of how students connect that knowledge to future endeavors beyond the schoolhouse gate" (2).

Conclusion

Tierney, Carter, and Desai (1991) believe, "Some of the values that underlie the use of portfolios include a belief in developing procedures for planning classroom learning that represents what students are actively doing; a commitment to student involvement in self-evaluation and helping students to become aware of their own development as learners; a belief in the view that assessment should take into consideration (1) the processes readers, writers, problem solvers, and learners enlist;

(2) the products they develop; (3) the improvements they achieve; (4) the effort they put forth; as well as (5) how these features vary across a range of learning experiences" (41).

We feel, along with many educators, that one of the most promising aspects of portfolio use is its ability to help students learn to reflect and self-evaluate. Self-evaluation often is met with skepticism because people confuse the concept with "giving oneself a grade." Typically, in school, students are told what is "good" work and what is "poor." Often they're not even told how to make anything better, since the product (not process) is what is being evaluated. Portfolios can be used as a method to teach students how to make judgments about their work, demonstrate growth, and even set goals for future learning.

Thoughts for Further Inquiry

1. Interview someone from another profession who uses a portfolio to showcase work (an artist, architect, model, advertising or marketing writer, etc.). Learn about how the portfolio was put together, its purpose, and why it's important to the professional. Who evaluates such a portfolio?
2. Choose something you've created of which you're pleased or proud (a piece of writing, a drawing, a tape of a musical performance). In writing, reflect on this product—why are you proud of it; what makes it good/important; what about the process that went into its production; what did you learn from it?
3. Prepare a portfolio that showcases you—as a writer, a teacher, a future teacher, etc. As you put your portfolio together decide how you will reflect on your choices and choose a format that will allow what you showcase to "speak for itself." Make sure this portfolio is authentic and serves a purpose in your life.
4. Discuss how you feel about the grading of portfolios. Can we justify giving grades for this type of product? If so, how can it be done?
5. An article published several years ago in an NCTE journal was titled, "Portfolios: Will Misuse Kill a Good Idea?" What do you think?

5

Grading: The Square Peg in the Round Hole

Papers are like people at a party. The A paper is the life of the party. Everyone wants to dance with the A paper. Most people wish the A paper was going home with them. The B paper isn't a great dancer, but tries real hard. The C paper is at the party, but sure ain't dancin'. The D paper decided not to show up. And the F paper didn't even know there WAS a party.

—Jennifer Brock, Texas A&M University Student

When we discuss the reporting aspect of assessment and evaluation, the first thing that comes to mind is the issue of grades, a practice steeped in tradition and politics. Grades are the one thing that the public thinks they understand and maintains a certainty that they want. They believe grades are a way to report what students are learning in schools. One set of parents we surveyed said, "Whether homework has been done or not and whether work has been performed with care or indifference have usually been discernible through the quarterly grades." Again, the objective, scientific principle leads the public and many educators to believe that grades refer to something definable—that grades are universal or they mean the same thing nationally, statewide, or at least locally. And yet, "parents make sense of a test score or a report card grade or comment based on their own schooling history, beliefs, and values. A test score may look 'scientific' and 'objective,' but it too must be

127

interpreted, which is always a subjective and value-laden process," contends the NCTE/IRA Joint Task Force on Assessment (1996, 5).

The Task Force further asserts, "When teachers write report cards . . . they must . . . represent a student's literate development in all its complexity, often within severe time, space, and format constraints. They must also accomplish this within the diverse relationships and cultural backgrounds among the parents, students, and administrators who might read the report. Some teachers are faced with reducing extensive and complex knowledge about each student's development to a single word or letter" (4).

Most teachers, when asked, say they have a difficult time distinguishing between evaluation and grading. Evaluation, the analysis of assessment data, is a judgment about learning or a summation of a learning experience. Grades are used more as a form of reward and punishment than as a true evaluation. Teachers evaluate, but so do students, their peers, and a combination of such interested parties. Teachers alone are given the responsibility of grading. When it comes to sharing that evaluation with the world (usually with parents, other teachers, and other institutions of learning), few others are involved, especially not the learners themselves.

Perhaps that is why grading generates the litany of laments: "If only we didn't have to give grades," "I'm worried that someone's going to mention I've given too many As and Bs," "I don't give grades—my students earn them," "This kid's parents are going to have a fit, but I'm sorry, this kid just isn't an A student."

Although awarding grades is by no means the only way of reporting, it is perhaps the most common practice in educational evaluation, and, most would agree, the most troublesome. The fact that grades are a flawed design is evidenced by how often we, in education, try to fix the design: new report cards, letter grades, percentages, weighted averages, and modified grades have all been used, reused, and rediscussed, but very little changes. We need to admit how little grades actually tell us. Stop any student in the hallway and ask her which teachers in the history department are the toughest graders. She'll rattle off names and then proceed to tell you who are the fairest and the easiest as well. None of these distinctions shows up on the report card. In the movie *Apollo 13*, the scientists and engineers in Houston are called upon to make a replacement part for the spacecraft, using only supplies available onboard, parts not designed for the task at hand. When engineers complained that it couldn't be done, they were told to make it work. They didn't have other options, they didn't have other parts, and they didn't have time. They had to make a square peg fit in a round hole. Grading, whether with letter grades or numbers, is a square peg in a round hole. Grading doesn't exactly fit in a transactional classroom with authentic assessment and evaluation, yet teachers have to grade. No matter how we assess and evaluate, for most of us, there comes a day when the Scantron sheets arrive in our mailboxes and we have to report grades. Like the *Apollo 13* engineers, we must find a way to supplement report cards with other information that explains grades and gives parents (and other interested parties) more information than just an 85 percent or a grade of B. Sending home supplements, such as rubrics, students' self-evaluations, and narrative comments that address the criteria for learning, will give parents a clearer picture of what their children are learning and what they are accomplishing.

Mixed Messages

Teachers around the country are being encouraged to try varied and alternate methods of assessment; we've already discussed rubrics and portfolios and other types of authentic and performance assessments. Are grades an explanation of product? progress? effort? achievement? growth? Each of these is a part of what we assess and evaluate in our classes and each has an impact on the learning process and what is learned, but a single grade obviously can't report all these things.

Traditionally, assessments consisted of tests, made up of mostly objective questions, and awarding grades was mostly a matter of averaging a number of individual test/assignment grades in a grade book—eight or nine a marking period, for example. But if techniques are to be used that drive instruction according to individual progress, how are teachers supposed to represent all that information with a single letter or number grade that somehow vaguely translates as superior, good, average, below average, and failing? If we think about these qualifiers, superior implies a comparison to that which isn't superior (and so forth). These qualifiers require teachers to compare students to something else: each other? past student performance? their own or others'? national or local standards? districtwide outcomes? If we look at most report cards, there is no explanation of the measurements superior, good, average, below average, and failing.

Kathleen goes to a doctor regularly for a back problem, and at the beginning of her appointment must rate how she feels on a scale from 1 to 10, a 1 meaning she can't get out of bed (absurd, considering she's in the office) and a 10 meaning she's feeling in perfect shape (and probably wouldn't be in the office). That seems reasonable enough, until we consider that the remaining eight numbers represent a general high (8–9), middle (4–7), and low (2–3). She could just as easily rate herself, good, bad, or so-so. Kathleen's been reporting scores in the 5, 6, 7 range, which is again not surprising, considering there are really no criteria for the numbers. In statistics, that's known as the tendency toward the middle. From the number given, her doctor can tell if she's feeling better or worse than her last visit, but then he could have done that by simply asking, "Feeling better?" The 1–10 scale gives an objective feel to the report, but there is no relationship between the numbers and the state of health. Grades in school operate in much the same fashion.

Measuring Ability

Grades are often perceived as a measure of ability—in fact, grades become definitions of who people are. All teachers have been guilty of referring to students as "A" students or "C" students, as if such grades define for the world who these people are, in terms of their accomplishments but more important as an overall definition of their ability, not just in school, but for life. If grades become who a student is, consider Renee's perception of herself when she receives grades of Ds and Fs in chemistry. On the first test in chemistry, the teacher told the class, "even a monkey could get 25." Renee got 24. Does this grade help Renee in her growth as a scientist? Does such a grade reflect the teacher's perception of Renee and ultimately Renee's perception of herself? Obviously, Renee learned to hate chemistry and learned she couldn't do it, being no smarter than a monkey.

It's difficult to overcome the odds, because many kids and their parents believe what grades supposedly tell them, and the kids become what schools expect them to be. As Diana Dreyer (1994) says, a "vicious cycle revolve[s] around dependence and grades, an interaction promoted by a numbers-driven culture overly reliant on measures that do not begin to address performance in context. . . . Students are all too aware of this grading phenomenon, an awareness leading to dependence . . . on the grade itself, a letter or number communicating to the world what kind of people they are and indicating what they are likely to become, a symbol ripe with ramifications for the present and the future, an extrinsic reward—or punishment—so overwhelming that we tend to overlook the intrinsic value of [learning]" (9). Ironically, grades don't define people in the real world outside of school. We could list the famous school failures who became successes—Einstein, Lincoln, Rockefeller—but when asked, everyone can think of someone who wasn't school smart (in other words, didn't get good grades), but who became extremely successful, exhibiting intelligence, even becoming leaders in their field once they left school. We all know "regular" people who were bright and overcame the odds, achieving more than their grades would predict.

My dad, Kathleen says, was one of those people; he was one of my finest teachers. I knew from the time I was a young child how "smart" my dad was. He watched the evening news every night, read magazines and newspapers, and taught me that an awareness of what was happening in the world was important. He taught me to think, resulting in periods where we could never agree, especially on anything political or religious. And even though I rarely agreed with him, I knew he would always be well prepared for our discussions. Although he never went to college or earned a degree, he taught himself cryogenic engineering, and taught others who had graduated from college how to make breathing units for extraterrestrial "outer space" and marine exploration. Was my dad smart? Obviously, I think so, but he always explained modestly that he never was much of a student, didn't do well in school, and joined the army during World War II as soon as he was old enough to enlist. School just had no place in his life. Did any of my dad's teachers assess his understanding or his potential? Did they know how much he knew about the world of plants and animals? ecology and forestry? physics and engineering? Of course not, because those weren't part of the curriculum.

In fact, teachers let my dad know how little they expected of him. I often heard him tell, years after it happened, the story of the history test he studied hard for (because it was interesting to him) and how he received a perfect score. Instead of congratulating him or capitalizing on this experience, his teacher accused him of cheating. Not only was such an accusation insulting, it told my dad that the teacher never expected him to get a good grade. Had she bothered to find out, that teacher would have known my dad loved American history and that he knew much more than her test was assessing. In some ways, my dad overcame the obstacles to learning that school put before him, but even if times had been different, I'm not sure my dad would have ever thought of himself as *school* smart or college material because no one in his school life let him demonstrate what he knew. We still look at learning with this limited perspective. We still report grades based on a competitive scale, comparing students in a class, those who seem to learn easily what the curriculum deems important, to those who seem unable to "get it," who seem lazy, or who seem not to care.

Measuring Achievement

Many look at grades as a report of achievement, a finite measurement taken at the end of a season, like the baseball standings. Each marking period seems to bring that period of learning to a close with the student expected to start again the next marking period. Grades are usually thought of as an end, not as a step. Since grades are incapable, where and how do we report progress, initiative, growth, and goals for future learning?

Most of the time achievement grades are used to "sort" students; in fact, we "categorize them so rigidly that they rarely escape" (Silberman 1970, 138). Regardless of whether they're reported as letters, percentages, or numbers, grades measure products, not usually process or progress. Alfie Kohn (1993) maintains that grades fail to provide students with valuable information; instead the process of grading causes students to concentrate on their performance rather than on their learning. He maintains, as do many of us, that the only legitimate reason for wanting to know how well students are doing—the only legitimate purpose for evaluation—should be to help them learn more effectively in the future. Grades, according to Kohn, dilute the pleasure that a student gets from working on and completing a task and also encourage cheating and strain the relationship of trust and respect between students and teachers.

As part of a journal entry, one of Kathleen's graduate students recovered a memory about writing poetry in high school that illustrates this point. Karen Patterson (1997) wrote,

> In high school, I would write my own private poetry and enjoyed doing it. When I was asked to do the same in school (in

junior and senior high school), I groaned. We always had to write a poem about something in particular. Or we had to write a particular type of poem. Also the thought of sharing these poems filled me with dread. It just did not seem to be the atmosphere for real writing. [Lucy] Calkins quotes the poet Naomi Shihab Nye that "you can't order a poem like you order a taco." My only somewhat positive experience with poetry in school came in my senior year in AP English. The teacher had us reading tons of poetry [written by] various poets from across the ages. We talked about the poems in circle discussion and whatnot. Then we had to write poems, and she didn't give us a topic. For the life of me, I cannot remember what my poem was about, but I still remember one of my classmate's poems. Jamie wrote a poem about her father who had passed away the previous year. It was so powerful; I remember her description of her emaciated father lying on a green mattress watching TV and waiting for death. Unfortunately this entire poetry experience was ruined for me by the teacher putting grades on these poems. Jamie got a B on her poem, and I felt that was so wrong. Her poem had real strength to it. I still remember it ten years later, but I can't remember even my own from that class.

If grades distort the experience of learning, how then do students become so grade conscious? Students learn to covet grades. Adults who are influential in their lives teach students through word and example that grades are important. Parents brag about their child's final grades; fast-food chains give prizes for "good" grades; students worry about whether "this will be on the final exam." Parents and teachers make comments such as, "What happened, Cindy? You dropped from an A to a B." And every student has heard the classic teacher admonition, "You'll have to work in my class; I'm a tough grader because I have standards." But the majority of students share the feeling that Katie Butler (1996), of Hempfield Area High School, shared with us: "I will always regard the grading of my written papers with a sense of dread."

Grappling with Gradelessness

Ohmer Milton, Howard Pollio, and James Eison (1986), in their book *Making Sense of College Grades*, say, "Faculty members have it within their power to reduce this pernicious and distorting aspect of educational practice that often seems to work against learning. If faculty would relax their emphasis on grades, this might serve not to lower standards but to encourage an orientation toward learning" (141).

Janine Rider (1996) of Mesa State College says that she tries to treat her students like real writers.

> I want them to start thinking of themselves as authors rather than as students doing more papers for another instructor. What really stifles this kind of thinking is grades. So I eliminate the problem—at least for fourteen weeks of the semester—by not giving grades. And the process works like a charm until the fifteenth week rolls around; the illusion fades and the need to record a final grade for the class stares us in the face. Then I wonder if there's any way to combine the illusion of gradelessness with the reality of final grades. Yet once I get through that last week and look at the semester as a whole, I know I'm committed to the ungraded papers approach. . . .
>
> I start the semester off with several weeks of writing bombardment: an assignment a night, including everything from a 150-word sentence to a dramatic monologue to a sonnet. We read our works aloud, we comment, but nothing gets turned in. This work becomes part of the semester's portfolio. Then come some more structured assignments like book reviews and opinion pieces, ending with a work of their choosing which is meant for publication. In fact, they turn it in to me in a stamped envelope, with a cover letter to an appropriate publication, and I mail it. We workshop two pieces per person. Everyone's piece-for-publication gets workshopped. In the meantime, I have conferences with the students, I read drafts, and I make abundant comments on their papers. They get plenty of feedback.

135

At the beginning of the semester, I give them the choice: grades on their papers, or no grades. Of perhaps one hundred students I've steered through the course, only one has chosen the grades. Ellyn was a nontraditional student and a perfectionist—as was apparent in her dress and grooming—and she didn't think she could stand not knowing her grade on each assignment. An excellent but nervous student, Ellyn ended up with a B in the class, and acknowledged that she was sorry she had voted to have grades. "I am too uptight not to know," she told me, "but not working for a specific grade might have loosened me up a little."

The others have unanimously expressed trepidation, then enthusiasm about getting back ungraded papers. Part of their portfolio is a letter to me which includes their assessment of their work, what grade they think they have earned, and why. Their letters let me know what the lack of graded papers provides for them. For example, Cathy was happy because she felt free to go "out on a limb with a very long and difficult final article" for her paper that we sent out for publication. Liz felt that the ungraded format "stretches a person and is fun at the same time." Wendi wrote, "I feel that college has taught me how to write for professors. This bothers me. The confidence that I lost in my writing was regained in this class."

The most common comment I see is that the ungraded format allows students to take risks in their writing. Some students actually found that they got so involved in the task of writing that they didn't even worry about whether it was A or C work.

Comments like these and the general enthusiasm of the class convince me semester after semester that I will never reinstate the graded paper into this class. Writers must take risks. The process of creating a fine work does not necessarily take place in the time frame demanded by a syllabus. Writers often write many lousy first drafts . . . [and] my students are delighted to discover that even famous writers have such drafts. [Considering the amount of] revision we do in class, they come to value those first and second and third drafts as much as their "final" products. I tried hard to encourage such "writerly" thinking during the semester. At the same time, we focused on writing for real, nonteacher audiences more than they had done before, emphasizing the goal of the carefully honed final copy.

Finally the Scantron grade sheet appears in my mailbox, and I know that the moment of truth is near. Actually, I find that students are pretty accurate in rating themselves. Seldom do I differ with their evaluation, and it's just as often to raise the grade of the too-humble as it is to burst the bubble of the hopeful. We agree on grades 80 percent of the time. What bothers me is how we each arrive at the grades. Julie said she would "be thrilled to receive an A. . . . I believe I have earned it based on the course requirements. To my knowledge I am missing no assignments, I have attended class sessions regularly (although I have missed a handful), and I have participated in class discussions." Jason wrote practically the same response: "I have done every assignment, and turned all of them in on time. I did not miss a single day of class, but I did not have much to say during classroom discussion. If my grade is based on the quality of my work, it should be a B. If it is based upon the quantity, my grade should be a B possibly a low A." Pennie was afraid to grade herself. Her writing was very good, but she admitted, "I did not write for fifteen minutes before each class. . . . I did not participate in class discussions." She realized that she hadn't done enough to merit an A.

But is an A to be given for attendance, participation, and work done on time? Or is an A to be given for super writing? And if it's for super writing, isn't it presumptuous to tell the students I'm not grading their papers and then give them a grade later based on the quality of those same papers? Certainly if I do so, all along I must have been thinking "This is an A (or B or C) paper."

Another problem is having final papers very different from one another. The piece Pennie chose to send off for publication was a carefully written three hundred-word humorous anecdote for a *Reader's Digest* column. How do I weigh this piece against Cathy's long, researched article for an education journal or Liz's humorous Alaska fishing adventure or Brandy's children's book? Are they equal? Does it matter, as long as each reflects the good writing expected for publication in that genre? My belief is that it doesn't matter; short concise pieces are often the most difficult to write. But the student [who has been] workshopping or [has turned] in a long, involved essay may balk at the short personal anecdote used by a fellow student to satisfy the same assignment.

It comes down to this in the fifteenth week: Every semester I think I'm being clear about how the grading works. I think the students will know if they are doing A or C writing and making A or C progress. I want to agree with them—unless, of course, disagreeing means telling a student she's getting an A instead of the B she suggested. Then I can bask in the glory of my "generosity," even though the work clearly deserved every bit of the good grade. I don't say in my syllabus "To get an A in this class, you must. . . ." Yet I always assume my agenda is not only clear, but continually clarified by the goals I set each day. This semester, a remarkable and thoughtful student put into one sentence what I try to get across over a whole semester. In her letter, Margaret told me, "As a person involved in education and struggling with assessment theories and practices, I think I would assess a student's work in a class by the growth she has shown from the start to the end and by the understanding or demonstration of the process of learning involved in the class." That's it, Margaret.

But there's no tool I know of that puts this kind of assessment on a one hundred-point scale, or that allows me to say ahead of time what constitutes an A or a C. Nothing's black or white; instead it's all shadowy greys. My assessment tool couldn't pass any reliability or validity tests. The assessment police may come stalking me. But until they do, I'm sticking with this murky method. I have felt fair in the grades I've given. Students haven't complained. Even Joanne, who figured she deserved a C but needed a B to help her GPA, wrote that "I know you will give me a grade that is fair, in any respect." She took her C graciously.

Margaret continued, "I feel I have been successful in this class. It has truly made an enormous difference in my life and in my confidence and in my writing. I have felt engaged in the assignments and have seen value in the accomplishment of them. . . . I have developed a visceral need to write that I intend never to lose. I guess this all means I deserve an A, although I feel as though the grade diminishes the true value of this class for me (I'll take it though)." I will continue to grade my class this way. (1–3)

Evaluation: Are Grades Necessary for Learning?

As we've said before, even well-intentioned teachers can draw the wrong conclusions from their ongoing assessments. For example, in an article recently published in *English Journal*, a twelfth-grade AP English teacher was disturbed by her students' claim that she was working them too hard (Mandrell 1997). She said her students were concerned about their grade point averages because they were taking hard courses instead of easy ones. The teacher decided that she would remove all grade pressure for one marking period by giving the students an automatic 98 percent and stressing learning for its own sake. All she asked was completion of the assignments, which would in turn prove that they were learning. What happened surprised and disappointed the students as well as the teacher. The students didn't read *Crime and Punishment* as was assigned and produced papers that were far from what they had the potential to produce. In their own reflections on the experiment, the students admitted that they needed a grade to push them to produce and that they were basically lazy procrastinators. The teacher's conclusion was that "learning must somehow be linked to a product. That product must be measured or graded to gauge the worth of the product according to the merit it deserves" (31). Obviously, this teacher will return to grading.

The teacher who wrote the article seemed to be a thoughtful, sincere educator, one who listened to her students and was willing to change for their sake. Despite all that, we think she missed the boat. As we read this article, we were amazed that the teacher didn't ask herself *why* the students didn't read the assigned readings. Had this teacher asked herself if the students in this class saw a reason to read *Crime and Punishment?* Learning, outside of school, is intrinsic. No one gave these students rewards if they learned to talk, to walk, to figure out how to build a Lego castle, or to find the constellations in the night sky. They learned these things because they had a purpose in their lives and they wanted to learn them. It was the teacher, not the students, who saw a "purpose" for the literary classic. She swooned, "I was not going to change my beautiful curriculum, resplendent with Dostoyevsky, Woolf, Camus, and Conrad" (28). The chosen work was near and dear to her heart, but hardly a part of her students' worlds. She never considered whether it was or how it could become so. Like the novel's title, her conclusion was that her students would only read with a promise of a reward for reading and a threat of punishment for not doing so. Is this learning? We don't think so, but using grades as a reward or punishment is certainly an easier way to motivate than to discover ways to open students' minds to difficult works and experiences and to facilitate learning in which students see a purpose. Even AP students have a difficult time entering Dostoyevsky's characters in nineteenth-century Russia, a world populated with paranoia and poverty. Why would they want to read *Crime and Punishment?* Learning for the sake of learning cannot be based on only the teacher's agenda and what the teacher feels is important to learn.

The Sabotage of Grading Competitively

Education is still under the spell of the bell curve—that mythical even distribution of something in which the majority of the population fell in the middle with a smaller number of subjects falling above or below the "norm." Many teachers, trained in this approach to achievement evaluation, still have a difficult time looking at students as individuals. They still look at evaluation as a comparison among a group, with the average falling somewhere in the middle and performance being judged as higher or lower than the norm. I remember, Kathleen says, receiving a memo one semester from the department chairperson with the grade distributions for all our undergraduate methods courses. Most students had received grades of As and Bs with fewer students receiving grades of C, D, or F. The memo asked the question, "Are our students really *this* good?" The implication, of course, was that we teachers had inflated our grades in some way because if a C grade were average then most of our students were graded above average. The problem, we believe, is with the entire concept of "average." What or who does average refer to? Kathleen teaches college juniors and seniors who, even to be accepted into the College of Education at our institution, had to achieve a B-minus or 2.5 grade point average in all liberal studies courses. When they enter her classes, they enter as students who have been relatively successful in college level courses. They enter to take their majors courses, the methods courses they have been waiting anxiously for. They are motivated, interested, and want very much to succeed in learning what they feel is most important in their preparation for their future career. As their teacher, Kathleen would hope that she taught well enough for the majority to meet their goals. Instead of grading them competitively, doesn't it make sense to grade them according to their demonstrations of learning, meeting the goals and criteria of the course?

"Too often we lead our students to believe that all that matters is how well they measure up to their peers," says Terrie St. Michel (1997) of South Mountain High School in Phoenix. "While it is true we live in a highly competitive society, we can best serve our students by showing them their own excellence and instill in them an intrinsic drive to improve, to continue to be better—for themselves" (2). John Krumboltz and Christine Yehn (1996) make the point with the title of their article, "Competitive Grading Sabotages Good Teaching," asserting that competitive grading hurts not only students but teachers by "turning teachers into students' opponents" (324). The very act of sorting and ranking students according to performance encourages teachers to look for weakness, error, and flaws. Assigning grades competitively turns teachers into critics and takes precedence over helping students succeed. To discriminate between students, teachers must resort to red-penning and counting errors. High school teachers worry that such sorting is necessary for colleges, but Krumboltz and Yehn warn against losing sight of what high school teachers are responsible for—supporting students as they reach their highest potential. The mission of high school is to teach teenagers, not to serve college admissions officers.

Krumboltz and Yehn claim that "competitive grading justifies inadequate teaching methods and styles" (324). It's ironic that the worst teachers seem to be the toughest graders. It's probably easier to blame students if they don't seem to be learning what teachers claim to be teaching. Krumboltz and Yehn would go so far as to say that "competitive grading rewards teachers for punishing students" (325). How often have we heard high school and university teachers boast that they give few As and many Ds and Fs in their classes because they have "high standards"? These teachers teach material that the students have little background in or purposely choose difficult material, not because it is important to the students' learning, but because it adds some kind of prestige to their course. These teachers believe all students should learn the same material in the same way at the same time for the sole reason that the teacher or the curriculum committee feels it's important. Teachers should never be congratulated or admired for failing the majority of their students or for giving low grades; the students are not to blame, the teacher is.

And yet, if every student in a class succeeded in meeting the objectives of the course, then each and every one would receive an A, a situation that the public, most teachers, and even students would deem unacceptable. Consequently, the system reinforces methods of assessment and evaluation that ensure that some students won't succeed. The teachers' choice of methods of instruction, their choice of evaluation instruments, and the amount of time and opportunities provided for students to complete tasks allows teachers to subconsciously set up barriers for students, thereby justifying teaching that fails to reach every learner. Competitive grading masks poor teaching because if some students are succeeding then, the reasoning goes, there must not be anything wrong with the instruction or the instructor. Grades that compare students with one another don't encourage students to do the best they can do; rather, they encourage students to do just enough to get by with the grade they have come to believe best describes them. Consequently many students do little to "stretch" themselves for an A, while others who see themselves as C students say, "Why bother? I'll never do as well as the 'smart' students."

Students in honors and gifted programs do well, in part, because of assumptions made about them and because of the nurturing care they receive from the best teachers (after all, they are the students that teachers aspire to teach). Similarly, the "special-admit" or "remedial" students do poorly, in part, because of the assumptions made about them and because of the lack of support their teachers receive.

Pressure to perform causes students to be concerned only with "what's on the test" instead of any interest in learning that connects to life or lifelong learning. The purpose of evaluation should be to help students understand what they can do and to help them set goals for future learning; instead, "competitive grading encourages methods of evaluation that misdirect and inhibit student learning" (Krumboltz and Yehn 1996, 325), making them think the objective of such courses is simply trying to figure out what will be on the final exam.

In misdirecting student learning, "competitive grading trivializes course content" (325). It's much easier to ask one-answer questions than to set up opportunities for students to make connections and to problem solve. It's much easier to quantify learning by dispensing knowledge and then evaluating the memorization of bits of knowledge. According to the NCTE/IRA Task Force on Assessment (1996), a major problem that occurs when we try to "align curriculum and assessment [is] that curriculum has reflected assessment rather than the other way around. Thus we have often achieved a trivial curriculum by aligning it with trivial assessments" (6). Evaluating understanding is more difficult because it requires not only that teachers consider the purposes and outcomes of a particular course of study when designing evaluation techniques, but also that they spend the time it takes to help students understand the goals and how those goals will be achieved.

A Matter of Respect

Grading has little purpose and surely no positive effects on learning unless there exists, between teacher and learner, an understanding of what both parties are responsible for. Grades are usually regarded as something that is *done* to students by teachers who are the *doers*. Much of this battle between teachers and students that results from grading also results in hostile interactions between teachers and students and teachers who look at students as lazy, unmotivated, and impossible to teach. Grades also can create a self-fulfilling prophecy, as a senior at Hempfield Area High School, Richard Kessler (1996), told us, "The number [at the top of the paper], whether written in red, black, green, or tangerine ink, dwarfs the teacher's comments about the text. . . . [And] if a student receives a poor grade, he may overlook the comments, opting to dwell on his overwhelming sense of complete and utter failure."

"Competitive grading deemphasizes learning in favor of judging. Learning becomes a secondary goal of education. Clearly then, the need to grade students undermines the motive—to help students learn—that brought most of us into the profession," say Krumboltz and Yehn (1996, 326). An ingredient that's often left out of the teaching/learning formula is that of respect. We've purposely avoided the horror stories that we've all heard or probably witnessed in our experiences as learners and teachers. We're going to share one such story, however, for the sake of illustration.

Glenn Wonsettler (1997) is a senior at a rural high school in Pennsylvania. Glenn tells the story of an experience he had with testing and grading a couple of years earlier:

> I went through the [Algebra 2] test and decided to do the last page first because it was easy, and I knew I could work [the problems] correctly and quickly. About halfway through the period, there was a fire drill. When students returned after the fire drill to finish working on the test, there were only three minutes until the period was over. When the bell rang dismissing students, the teacher said we could have the next day to work on the test, but the next day she gave us back the first page corrected and only allowed us to work on the last page which I had already completed. I ended up with a "D" on the test, which really pulled my grade down—not because I didn't know how to work the problems, but because my test-taking strategy—do the problems I know really well and am sure to get right first—was the opposite of how that test worked.
>
> When I explained my situation to the teacher, she said it was my problem, that I should've gone through the test in order, start to finish, front to back. It wasn't my lack of knowledge that earned my D that term—it was a teacher's rigid system of correcting papers—and I'm not sure what that has to do with learning, or for that matter, teaching. (1)

We said this was a horror story. It's obvious that such evaluation has more to do with control and power than with understanding what Glenn knew about algebra. More than demonstrating one teacher's lack of understanding about teaching and learning, we believe this shows the ingredient missing that is essential in the teaching/learning process: respect. Glenn's teacher showed no respect for Glenn as a person and a learner in the classroom. She treated Glenn in a way that was devoid of fairness and interest in Glenn as a person as well as an algebra student. Respect is as essential in evaluation as it is in teaching.

Esther Broughton (1997), who teaches at Mesa State College in Colorado, finds that how she regards her students affects both her teaching and ultimately the students' learning. It's obvious that Glenn's experience could never happen in Esther's classroom. Esther explains:

> With almost thirty years of grading experience, I still find myself agonizing over grades. Is grading difficult because my brain is filled with conflicting bits of wisdom? Do I fear judging lest I be judged? Do I fear being labeled as an "easy" teacher? Am I personally responsible for the national lowering of standards when I give a D to a student who attended every class, spent hours in the writing center, and still wrote an incomprehensible final essay? Is it possible to be both encouraging and objective? I'm embarrassed to admit that for the last few years my grading has been influenced by a television commercial popular perhaps ten years ago. A bubbly Florence Henderson of Brady Bunch fame bounced before the camera and offered this advice for successful dining: Treat your family like guests and your guests like family. I've modified the adage: I try to treat my first-year composition students like senior English majors.
>
> But wait, I hear my cynical colleagues say, there's a world of difference between these two groups. Senior English majors know why they're in school; first-year composition students frequently flounder. Senior English majors profess enthusiasm for the course content; first-year composition students confess they're in class because English is a graduation requirement. What's more, senior English majors are regularly in seminar-sized classes of fifteen to twenty students; first-year composition classes number thirty students. In spite of the validity of some of

these comparisons, I know that my expectations for my composition students will affect the way they write and I grade.

I admit that I do nothing out of the ordinary. I have no foolproof method that will always be the most efficient and effective instrument for senior English majors or first-year composition students. I've experimented with portfolios, point systems, letter-writing, journals, scoring rubrics, holistic grading, and, yes, even Scantron multiple-choice tests.

Ultimately, the principle that guides my grading is remaining open to new ideas about assessment. I keep a grading folder with ideas for improving grading. These suggestions come from reading books and articles, talking with my colleagues and students, attending conferences, and keeping class notes from one semester to the next.

For both senior English majors and first-year composition students, I need to make my grading procedures explicit and direct. The final section of my syllabus reveals the guidelines I've set for the course. In addition to the syllabus, prior to each major assignment, my students and I—the seniors and the freshmen—construct criteria for grading that assignment.

First-year composition students and senior English majors need to stay informed. I write brief progress reports to my classes three or four times each semester. The report addresses issues that pertain to the whole class. I ask for individual progress reports returned to me by the students explaining their efforts, asking questions, making suggestions. I encourage students to write, e-mail, call, or come by my office any time they desire. (Yes, some days I spend a good amount of time answering e-mail.)

Last of all, I try to be as generous with praise with my composition students as I am with my senior English majors. The praise must be honest, but I've found it easy to follow Donald Murray's lead and start my reactions to student essays with the phrase, "One thing I like about this piece is the way. . . ." While I may occasionally forget the wisdom provided by Florence Henderson, student feedback helps me to remember its importance. A letter from a senior English major in a classical rhetoric class contained the following paragraph:

"I wanted to write you one last time. I don't have any news relating to rhetoric or any great authors. Mainly I wanted to mention that you were very important to my sister. She was in one of your first-year composition classes four or five years ago. She told me how supportive you were of her. I didn't find out until recently that [the same person] she used to tell me about was who I was taking a class from. . . . I just wanted to let you know that you may not even know when you are completely affecting a student's life."

That's the kind of morale-boosting message that makes me sure that treating my first-year composition students like senior English majors is worth the effort. (1–3)

If we return to the purpose of assessment and evaluation, we have to agree with Esther's premise. Tina Shorr (1996), a teacher at Karns City Area High School in Pennsylvania, told us that she's learned when grading "to always err on the side of compassion." Expecting success, looking for the positive, and providing support nourishes learners and sustains the learning process. Assessment or evaluation has to be respectful—it has to support students, not degrade or punish them. It has to be honest, understandable, and purposeful. We hope Glenn experiences a teacher like Esther or Tina soon.

Thoughts for Further Inquiry

1. Discuss the issue of grading. What do grades stand for? How can teachers use grades to support students? What are students' roles in grading?
2. Interview teachers about their grading policies. How are grades determined in their classes? Are they satisfied with the school's grading policy? Have they changed how they grade over the years? How do first-year teachers feel about grading? Did their undergraduate courses prepare them for

this part of the evaluation process?

3. Look at research on grading. How is it defined? Has its emphasis changed over the years? Does research support the use of grades? According to research, how do grades support or hinder students?

4. Look at report cards from a number of school districts. What are their strengths/deficiencies? How are they similar? As a teacher, which one would be easiest for you to use? why? most difficult to use? why?

5. Many schools have report card committees. Join such a committee or talk with someone who is a member. What are the issues being addressed? Are teachers moving toward report cards that will support learners? be based on defined criteria? look at individual strengths and student goals? What is driving the perceived need to change report cards?

6

Teachers Aren't
the Only Players

The checklists tell me more about what my son can do,
but I still want a grade. I need to know how he's doing in
comparison to others in his grade.
—Anonymous response from a parent on questionnaire

The "game" of assessment and evaluation is crowded with players: parents, administrators, community members (including
those on school boards), teachers, and students. Parents, community members, and even administrators are usually thought
of as recipients of reports, but they sometimes have a more
active voice in assessment and evaluation.

Part of our culture celebrates the idea of "sameness." We
know parents want their children to walk at the same age
(about the "average" of one year), to talk at the same time their
peers do, and to be able to do what some authority deems
"appropriate" at a certain time in life. Books such as the popular *What to Expect from Your Infant* reassure parents that their
child is progressing "normally," even though the premise of
most books of this type is that many things are "normal." When
children are ready for school, parents look to E. D. Hirsch Jr.'s
Core Knowledge Series and the book sequence, *What Your
First-Grader Needs to Know*, *What Your Second-Grader Needs to
Know*, etc. These books, unlike the ones parents read to help
them through their child's infancy, suggest to parents that there
are things *all* children should know at certain ages in their lives.

Anyone who knows about developmental theories of learning would understand how preposterous this concept is, but parents and most of the general public have been led to believe that there really are levels of achievement that can be measured in years or grade levels. This thinking is so prevalent that hardly anyone questions the validity of the artificial grade levels that have been used in American schools, from first grade to twelfth, or the notion of using passing or failing as rewards or punishments for achievement in any given year. These notions are simply embraced as *a priori* truths, along with other beliefs, such as the concept of the "average" performance, or statement of what a typical tenth-grade student should and ought to do. Unfortunately, such achievement is commonly measured by criteria that parents are either unsure of or consider vague. Sadly, most don't care about the exact criteria, just so long as their son or daughter "measures up."

Parents' Right to Choose

President Clinton said that he and Vice President Gore are committed to ensuring "that parents are an active part of their children's learning all the way through school." One of the initiatives he promised was to "give parents the power to choose the right public school for their children," believing that competition "can make public schools better" ("State of the Union" 1997). This well-intentioned promise, like those made by proponents of charter schools and vouchers, sounds like the choice that Monty Hall gave contestants: what's behind door number 1, door number 2, or door number 3. As a parent, you make a choice and hope it's a good one.

When we were moving to Pittsburgh, we tried to exert "the power to choose the right public school" for our daughter. We asked the admissions office at the university to name the school districts they considered the best. We looked at statistics such as the percentage of graduates in a school district who continued with their education. When we identified what looked to be a good school district and phoned to make an appointment to speak to someone about the specifics of the program, we were told that we couldn't have an appointment until we had purchased a home in the North Allegheny school district. We had better luck at a neighboring district, one whose writing program was being rewritten because of their association with the National Writing Project. The language arts coordinator was more than gracious about spending an afternoon with us discussing the North Hills School District and allowing us to speak to students. On the basis of that experience, we chose to buy a home in the North Hills district. People we told about our decision replied with two pieces of information, almost said in the same breath: It was a good school, though it didn't have North Allegheny's reputation, and that their football team was first in the nation the previous year. We're afraid that in the absence of any real information, parents' "power to choose the right public school" will always be compromised by having to rely on incomplete and quantified evaluations: test scores, teacher-student ratios, grading statistics, and extracurricular marketing bonuses such as the number of clubs and sports teams (and their standings), dress codes, and security.

Parents' Desire to Help

Many parents are interested in the daily progress of their children and express a desire to be more involved in their son or daughter's education, actively helping to support their children. In a survey sent to a range of parents of high school children, we found that most said they were satisfied with the present traditional grading systems in their secondary schools and with simply a report of *how well* their son or daughter was doing in school. When we asked parents on our grading survey how much information they felt grades gave them as parents, the system they seemed satisfied with, one parent gave a cryptic reply: "On a scale of 1–10, a 5," perhaps to show us how little information a 5/10 actually gives. Another set of parents thought a percentage grade told more than a letter grade, but didn't elaborate. Other parents thought grades "generally mirrored motivation and effort" and that the "comments on work performance as well as grades" gave them the information they needed. Still others had the opposite reaction, believing "that grades give a partial picture of what is accomplished each day in the classroom. . . . [Since] each teacher takes different criteria into consideration when calculating grades (i.e., some use homework scores, some use class participation, others just use test and quiz scores)" or that grades are inaccurate—"not indicative of ability" and unsatisfactory, telling "very little about whether my son is doing his work or not."

A pair of parents mentioned that the process whereby grades are determined is a mystery and that grading is "tricky" because sometimes it's a measure of effort, sometimes a measure of what students know. So mysterious are grades perceived to be that we heard similar stories from parents from different school districts. The truth behind grading is revealed when the students prove what many have long suspected: The teacher grades according to how well he/she likes the students. Parents told us their children had swapped assignments with classmates and "the students have found that different grades are given to the same pieces of writing depending upon the name on the paper."

As varied as these responses were, the parents seemed to be looking for many of the same things that report cards have been unable to provide. Parents want to know about types of learning such as depth of thinking and abstract reasoning. Is the classroom activity truly meeting the child's needs? Parents want to know about social learning: their child's ability to get along with others and how well they work in groups. Parents were interested in learning how students performed in group learning experiences (did they emerge as leaders or followers) and how they cooperate. Parents want to know about effort made and working up to potential. Where can improvement be made? Do they spend enough time on task? Parents want teachers to communicate real information to them so parents can feel they have a picture of what's happening during the seven hours that their sons and daughters are in school.

What Did You Get?

Parents want to know about interpretations of the grade—what it means. How are tests and quizzes weighted against home-work? How do grades relate to specific goals or objectives? How do their children compare to classmates? Some felt the teach-ers' perspective of what a particular grade means was totally dif-ferent from theirs.

It's interesting to note that many parents still want to know what the grade distribution in that class was and where did his/her child fall in the distribution? In other words, they want to know how their son or daughter is doing in comparison with others in the class. That shouldn't surprise us since the system of education in American schools remains competitive: class rank, honor rolls, etc. From their own experiences in school, parents themselves learned that schooling is competitive—good grades got you schol-arships and entrance into exclusive universities. Grades gave you power, and what parent doesn't want to empower his/her child, at least in his/her preparation for the adult world? Would parents be happy if all students in their child's class received an A or a B? We think most parents would interpret it to mean grade inflation. Fewer parents would interpret it to mean that all the students were interested in learning and were successful with a teacher who did a good job of supporting them until they reached a suc-cessful level of performance. Most would probably see the lack of stratification as meaning that the teacher was too easy, too lazy, too liberal, and too experimental, and that those grades don't mean as much as ones that produced a bell curve.

Another thing we learned through our conversations with parents is that they want information, often more than grades will tell them. Some had suggestions for what that might mean—seeing work in progress, having more information about effort, criteria, assignments, and progress—but most were unsure of how this could be done. Other parents reported that they believed standardized tests like the SAT really told them more than grades. Such comments reaffirm the trust the public has in national testing companies, such as the Educational Testing Service (ETS), and show to what extent the media have convinced the public that standardized tests do much more than they actually do, or were intended to do.

Communication Specialists

Parents went on to report that there was very little communication between teacher and parent at the secondary level beside the report card. As teachers, do we encourage parents to become involved, or do we shut them out? Parents would like to be involved, but by the time their children are in secondary school, parents are afraid they can't really help, due to the complexity of the curricular content, the developing of adolescent independence, and the absence of a place for parental involvement. Neither the students nor the teachers expect parents to do the homework or provide the answers. Parents don't have to remember geometry in order to help at home.

Parents can help by talking about assignments and by providing the right conditions and encouragement helpful to learners. Parents can foster independence by listening to how their child approaches a problem or assignment, even if the content is unfamiliar, and by giving their child a chance to "think aloud." Such involvement passes no judgments and makes no evaluations, but provides the encouragement that students need, and it demonstrates to students that their parents are truly interested in what they're doing and learning.

Barbara King-Shaver (1996) requires her students at South Brunswick High School in New Jersey to "develop a mentoring team of adults from both inside and outside of school. Parents and guardians are encouraged to participate as mentors, and they are invited to join in the intellectual challenges of their children at several parent meetings" (1).

As educators we have a responsibility to involve parents in their child's education, and sometimes that means bringing the school to them. The important thing is connecting teachers, students, and parents in nonthreatening and positive ways. Since almost all homes have VCRs, conferences can be video-taped with both the student and the teacher addressing the parent throughout. Projects, debates, plays, and presentations can be videotaped, with students describing to parents what they're seeing and why it's important. Tapes can be purchased for each student and shared (less cost than most report card systems, Scantrons, or other supplies that are commonly used). In high schools, teachers who respect parents' abilities to support students at home can involve parents in what's going on in the classroom through better communication.

Conferences Involving Parents and Students

The parents we spoke with mentioned that although satisfactory progress reports exist in some schools, these reports seem to be sent home only when performances or behavior are unsatisfactory. Parents told us that parent-teacher conferences were held only if there was a severe problem, or if required by law, for example as part of an Individualized Education Plan (IEP). Most parents seemed to think that more conferences should be scheduled, but some who have attended conferences reported that the conference didn't tell them much; the teacher just reviewed report cards and standardized test scores.

It seems strange that when we conference about a student's progress or achievement, we traditionally do so without the student being present. Kathleen says she can remember waiting for her parents to return from parent-teacher nights. Her first question was always, "What did they say about me?" She says she really had no idea what her teachers really thought of her.

Many teachers are working on ways to involve students in

the traditional parent-teacher conferences, such as having students lead them. After all, students are not only capable of leading conferences, but are in the best position to do so. In schools where students lead conferences with their parents or other interested adults, class time is provided prior to the conferences for discussion of format considerations and other possibilities. The students prepare ahead of time for the experience: They gather materials, prepare self-evaluations of criteria that are understandable and predetermined, recognize their individual strengths and needs, and set goals for their immediate future in the class. Such conferences are often held in the evening so more parents can attend. Initial reaction is often skeptical because parents are used to hearing "reports" from teachers. However, when they have an opportunity to hear how much their son or daughter knows about their own learning and how they can articulate where they hope to go, parents are better able to determine how they can best support their child.

It is important that teachers provide ground rules before the night of the conferences. Letters can be sent home explaining the purpose and procedures as well as rules for participation. Parents must be made aware of the importance of self-assessment and reminded that every student is an individual with different abilities and needs. Such letters can make it clear that the student will be honest and will be looking for support and encouragement, not empty praise or harsh criticism. This is not a time to criticize, belittle, or discourage. Teachers may still need to provide time for individual parent-teacher-student conferences, but even those conferences might best involve the student.

Broadening Parent Awareness

Cathy Fleischer (1997), a teacher educator at Eastern Michigan University, believes it's unfair to expect that parents know what teachers know about process writing or transactional classrooms. We have to have patience when we communicate with them and have to educate them as well. Cathy believes teachers need to be proactive before problems arise. As her husband suggests, teachers might begin to think like community organizers and take a lesson from public awareness groups like Mothers Against Drunk Driving (MADD). Cathy believes teachers could broaden parents' awareness to include evaluation of whole programs rather than simply the relative rank of their own children.

One of the teachers Cathy works with, Carolyn Berge (1997), takes the proactive stance. At open house, Carolyn gives each parent a piece of a jigsaw puzzle as they come in the room; they're told to look at their piece and the others around them and to try to guess what the jigsaw picture is. After guessing, she shows them the completed jigsaw picture and says that education is like a puzzle—you can't guess the big picture from just one or two pieces or methods of testing—you have to look at the whole child. Her homework assignments regularly involve the family, including asking parents and grandparents to read together with students and act as resources for homework assignments. Carolyn maintains a parent library where she lends professional books and journals to parents that explain what she's doing in her program. She believes this gives her credibility.

Another teacher associated with Cathy Fleischer, Kathleen Hayes-Parvin (1997), invites parents to read the class book of writings by sending the book home with a different student each night, attaching a sheet explaining what to look for in the writings and asking that parents write a response that will be added to the growing book. Parents are also invited to write for the class book, with no restrictions as to length or topic.

We realize that the level of parental involvement differs within schools and within districts and neighborhoods. Not all parents look to schools as friendly places, due to their past experiences and less-than-fond memories of school years. These parents often see teachers as the enemy; they send their kids to school because it's the law. Open house? The notice goes in the trash, if it ever gets home. Conferences? What can *they* do if teachers can't do their job? It's not that such attitudes reflect a lack of love or caring, but rather a kind of helplessness in a system that often fails those whom it should help the most.

Cathy Gwizdala (1997), a third teacher Cathy Fleischer works with, realizing that school is sometimes an uncomfortable place for her students' parents to visit, holds social functions for the parents, for example, evening celebrations and holiday parties held at times when the school is normally empty. School becomes "an evening out." Cathy uses this time to perform what she thinks of as inservice for unaware parents—she fills the halls and walls with displays of completed works and works in progress; she plays videotapes of the students presenting their work to each other in class. The parents' evening out becomes a way to see school and school work in a positive light.

Messages Adults Give: Rewards, Bribery, Punishment

A recent feature story in our local newspaper, titled "Gunning for Better Grades" (1997), disturbed us on many levels. The writer explained that her son had developed an interest in hunting, our area's favorite pastime, after relatives had ignored her wishes that her son not be given toy guns. (So avid are hunters in our area that the first day of deer hunting season is a school holiday, but not Veteran's Day, Columbus Day, or presidents' birthdays.) The writer went on to explain that no punishment or reward had yet instilled in her son, a poor speller, a lasting desire to improve his spelling grades—until now. Depending on how well he did on his spelling tests, her son was given money to save to buy the gun he wanted for hunting; she called it gunning for grades. The son's grades improved; he was happy, his parents were happy, his teachers were happy, and probably the only unhappy ones were the deer hiding in the area woods, who come November will have to escape the shots of yet another sixteen-year-old hunter (we hope that he's a better speller than marksman).

This is a parent with the best intentions for her son, doing what she can to provide him with a reason to care about his spelling, something his teachers hadn't been able to do. We won't even try to deal with the wisdom of spelling tests as a measure of language use or the appropriateness of giving a gun to a young person, but we would ask teachers to consider what message external rewards give to students about learning: Learning is so repugnant that one must be bribed to engage in it.

Before school, children look out their bedroom window at night and ask questions like, "Mommy, where does the moon come from?" This type of question comes from a genuine desire to understand how the world works. Both Frank Smith (1988) and Alfie Kohn (1993) point out that learning is a natural part of our lives and that rewards are not a necessary end-product of learning. Curiosity is natural in young children and students, like Heather Meloy (1997), a student at Derry Area High School outside Pittsburgh, who expressed it this simply: "Last year I took an astronomy class Mr. Feather taught. I have always had a deep interest in the subject and genuinely enjoyed the class. Mr. Feather played on my deep curiosity and often started class discussions where everyone was involved." Learners are more apt to learn if they are interested and invested in what they are learning. The intrinsic rewards of the learning experience itself are what encourage us toward further learning; the satisfaction of knowing is the reward we naturally expect— unless we have been "trained" to expect something else. Such learning is natural until adults, usually parents and teachers, convince learners somehow that learning must be painful because they need rewards for "doing it" and a threat of punishment if they don't. In secondary school, those rewards and punishments take the form of grades. The use of reward systems results in a loss of satisfaction and excitement that comes from the learning experience itself.

The extrinsic reward can never be as satisfying as the intrinsic reward. Jeff Golub, of the University of South Florida, tells the parable of an old man who was harassed daily by children on their way to school, a story he borrowed from Alfie Kohn (1993). The old man grew tired of shouting requests that the children stop their taunts. One morning he called after the children, telling them if they would come back the next morning and repeat their insults, he would give each child a dollar. The children came back the next morning and, true to his word, the old man gave them each a dollar. Then he said that if they'd come back the next day, each would receive fifty cents. The children came back and, after shouting the required insults, received their fifty cents. The man seemed pleased and told them that the next day he would give each child a quarter. The children came back the next day, though not as many as before, and as he gave them their quarters, he promised them each a shiny new dime if they'd insult him the next day. One boy looked him and said, "Are you kidding? This ain't worth no dime, man." The old man was never bothered again.

There are those who would counter that our school systems also use grades as a form of reward and punishment to get students to learn. Alfie Kohn (1993), author of *Punished by Rewards*, certainly believes so: "Rewards are used constantly in nearly every classroom to try to motivate children and improve performance. They are offered stickers and stars, edible treats and extra recess, grades and awards. New goodies are substituted as students get older, but the Skinnerian formula follows them. Often they are rewarded for getting rewards: A good set of grades means a place on the honor roll, perhaps a special ID card, a basket of freebies at local stores, and even cash from parents " (143). The expectation "what will you give me if I do this" is a result of students being forced to learn what isn't interesting or valuable in their eyes, and the promise that if they "play the game" and do as they are told, they will get a reward. Even Skinner's pigeons wanted the food pellets they were trained to get, but often students see no purpose for the curriculum that we mandate.

Too many parents and students are conditioned to believe that students need such motivators in order to learn. As one student revealed, "I need the letter grade to keep me in line, I use the grade as discipline . . . I need the security of a letter grade to tell me that I'm doing well and to tell me that I'm a good student" (Clawson 1996, 7).

Administrators: A Part of the Team?

Administrators are often looked upon as company directors who are interested in grades only for the role they play in public relations or in making judgments about their teachers.

Too many administrators are more concerned with the politics of grading and testing than in the purpose or effect of evaluation. One teacher in Kathleen's graduate class told us that in her first year of teaching, her principal ignored her until after the first marking period. At that time, he paid a visit to her room after school to discuss the fact that she was being "too easy" on her students—she had given too many A's and B's on their report cards. It didn't seem to matter that he knew nothing of what was going on in that classroom or what criteria were being used to assign grades; the absence of a bell curve meant only one thing: grade inflation. Other teachers in her building also told her to "toughen up" her grading system, for her own sake. The teacher was confused and frightened. She knew things were going well; the kids were excited about learning in her class, working hard, and almost all meeting criteria that were reasonable, clear, and appropriate. How could she award "lower grades"? Although the principal seemed to be pleased with her performance throughout the year, they were never able to resolve the problem of her "easy grading."

Not all administrators take this view, although the public pressure for traditional bell curve grading systems is pretty strong in most districts. Nevertheless, we found a growing number of administrators who were not only interested in learning how to make assessment and evaluation more understandable to their teachers but were themselves struggling with rethinking the role that assessment and evaluation play in their schools, individual classrooms, and in the community. Many administrators have worked hard to provide opportunities for teachers to learn more about assessment and evaluation by providing inservices, consultants, and even have recommended the payment of workshops and graduate courses for teachers who they hope will act as change agents. Ironically, in many school districts, the administrators don't actually participate in any of these experiences themselves. They don't often get involved in regular meetings and work sessions as a part of a team, working together with teachers to make sense of a complicated issue. And the fact is, teachers need more than administrative support; they need administrative involvement.

Community

Community perceptions about assessment and evaluation are always difficult to influence. One of the things that everyone believes they understand about education is grades. They're accepted as an appropriate measure of achievement and the proper reward or punishment by a society that endorses the behaviorist orientation of schools as "what they are and what they should be." When we speak with people outside the education community about grades and evaluation, we often hear the echo of Kathleen's mother's favorite expression: "The old ways were the best ways." Well, we'd argue that the old ways may not be best, but they are as comfortable as a pair of worn-out slippers and just as difficult to get rid of.

Cathy Fleischer (1997) suggests that teachers enter into the dialogue of the community by acting as resource persons for the local newspaper, as contact people to provide responses or explanations whenever there is an education story being written. Cathy also suggests teachers write op-ed pieces for their local papers explaining their views of national or local education issues. Carol Jago, a teacher at Santa Monica High School and the director of the California Literature Project at UCLA, believes parents and community members can make informed decisions about public education only if they are informed. Carol does her part by writing a weekly column for her local community newspaper. Her articles are so timely and so well received that her work has been picked up by major daily newspapers such as the *Los Angeles Times*. Because public education is funded by the public, the community will always be involved in the evaluation of programs and policies. Carol and Cathy argue that teachers need to ensure that teachers' perspectives get heard.

So often the bad press educators and schools receive is based on misconceptions and untruths. Teachers have to make sure the public is aware of what is really going on. Sometimes our community role can be simple. We can get the word out through the students. We can contact local banks and shopping malls and arrange to have our students' work displayed for the community at large. We can let people see the great things our students are doing in classrooms and these products will be evidence of the learning that is taking place in our classrooms.

The Students' Role in Assessment and Evaluation

As soon as a discussion of students' involvement in their own learning is begun, the discussion quickly dissolves into the issue of whether students should be grading themselves. We don't believe so, but before tackling the question of who grades and what the process will be, the discussion must return to the issue of what learning is and how it is best supported.

As we've said, the purpose for assessing students' progress is to help the student discover "where to go next" and help the teacher support that growth. If learning is to be ongoing, then helping students understand how an evaluative judgment is made and how to reflect on the progress of their own learning can only help them look at what's still needed to learn to accomplish their goals. Evaluation, although it involves judgment, is not necessarily final. Teachers like Jane Cowden (1996) always make the self-evaluation tied to the goals the students have set for themselves and will set for reading and writing.

Bill Clawson (1996), a teacher at Santa Monica High School in California, has taught Homer's *Odyssey* to high school sophomores for twenty-five years in what he calls "an array of configurations such as remedial, typical, accelerated, gifted, and nowadays 'honors.'" Bill discovered that students have a variety of perceptions about evaluating and grading and that letting them reflect on their own performance can be a learning experience for both the teacher and the students. Bill explains:

> I would "teach" the first twelve books of the *Odyssey*, filling in background about the characters and the gods and goddesses. Next, I would assign teams of students to each of the remaining books of the *Odyssey* and require them to "teach" that book to the rest of the class. I have witnessed everything from a short speech followed by a three-question true/false test to a costumed major movie studio type production, with an Odysseus lashed to the mast of a galley ship, tempted by the school's madrigal singers posing as the sirens.
>
> But lately, I have been thinking a lot about authentic assessment and testing, and I wondered what is the value of testing about Homer. . . . One alternative strategy that had proved very successful . . . was to take an episode . . . write about it briefly, and then construct an opening question for a Socratic seminar. For example, one highly charged seminar started with the question, How are the Lotus Eaters like modern drug sellers? The episode fell on the same week that we had a schoolwide drug-free program, complete with red ribbons. Following the Kyklops episode, we discussed the ways in which the Kyklops embodied everything contrary to Greek civilization. . . . I had modeled all

the meaning-making strategies I could to teach the book. We mapped Odysseus' progress; we diagrammed relationships; we dramatized certain readings; we drew symbols for actions; and we diagrammed and wrote about such things as leadership ability and the Greek idea of *arete* or virtue. When the time came to give the assignment for the students to teach their part of the book, I called it a presentation. (1–2)

Bill's assignment asked students to make a dramatic or academic presentation to the class (from twenty to forty minutes) in which they would explain any parts of the book that they found difficult and interpret any symbolic actions or events, relating them to Greek life or the present day. Furthermore, Bill asked them to provide a written summary for the class and ask an essay question as homework or classwork, which would then be graded by them with comments on the writing.

After giving the assignment, Bill says that he

circulated around and conferenced with groups about what they might do. The groups talked to each other and coordinated their plans so that they didn't duplicate each other. When the presentations began, we tried to do two a day. After reading Alfie Kohn's (1993) book, *Punished by Rewards,* in which Kohn demonstrates how instant rewards destroy intrinsic motivation, I was somewhat distressed by the number of quiz shows the students devised in which candy was given as a reward for answering questions. Nevertheless, I began to feel pretty good about what was happening when I saw the ingenuity they used to devise their Jeopardy games, the lengths they went to to devise apparatus for their shows, and the out-and-out fun everyone seemed to be having. I was especially heartened to see some groups try to conduct a small Socratic seminar as had been done during the reading of the first half of the book. They did puppet shows, videotaped dramatizations, an academic lecture that required a great deal of research, and a heated discussion conducted by two energetic young women about the sexual double-standard for men and women in Homer's day. Then it came time for assessment. My students had had some fun, but really they were dying to know their grades.

I had been reading about portfolios and authentic assessment in an article by Grant Wiggins (1989b). Wiggins had said, "a test must become more than an indicator of one superficial symptom. . . . A test must offer students a genuine intellectual challenge" (705). Wiggins wanted teachers to ask how the results of a test would help students know their strengths and weaknesses on essential tasks. What kinds of challenges will have the most educational value for students? (2)

Bill devised a self-assessment for the students on their presentation of the *Odyssey*. Bill's directions to the students were

Write a report on every phase of your presentation of the *Odyssey*. Design your own format for this report and type it. Consider the following things: How much time did you spend? How well did you and your partners get along? Briefly outline what your plan was. What was your unique contribution to the plan? What was your partner's contribution to the plan? What part of the plan came as a result of teamwork? How well did the class understand and learn from your presentation? What was the intellectual level of your plan? What was the *fun level* of your plan? Do you think that you learn anything when you have fun (does anyone, for that matter), or does most learning come by hard work and discipline (and should that discipline come from yourself or from someone else)? Did you learn anything about working with another person? Did you learn anything about the *Odyssey* that you didn't know before?

[The assignment continued,] Write a paragraph or two about the question, Should students be graded on effort or accomplishment? (Remember: Would you want your brain surgeon to be graded on effort or accomplishment?) Interview two people in the class and ask them what they remember about your presentation and what they thought of it. Try to get them to be specific. Write up the interview. All things considered, what grade would you give yourself? Explain in some detail why you assigned yourself the grade you did.

The results of this self-assessment turned out to be more interesting than I had dreamed. First, I must stress that I said that this was not to be an essay but a report. I showed the students . . . reports from corporations with graphs and facts and figures . . . to entice them to use their computer knowledge, beyond word processing, to do a newsletter format. I completely underestimated the creative urges and competitiveness of the students. . . . Most of the reports were done in folders and some were put into intricate computer forms that required a sophisticated knowledge of software and software manipulation. But the display reports that started showing up just before Christmas vacation were dazzling. . . . One was a giant gift-wrapped box with many smaller gift-wrapped boxes inside it. Each smaller box had a question taped to the outside and on the inside was the typed answer. Another was a small Christmas tree with lights and ornaments made out of egg shells, colored and decorated with ribbons and braid, and each egg had an opening, inside which was a tiny scroll of paper tied with a red ribbon. And, yes, the answer to each question was on the scroll. I could go on about the poster with a big "right brain" and "left brain" with the appropriate questions typed on them and a huge "self-assessed brain" with the remaining questions answered. But let these examples suffice. (3–4)

Without Effort, You Can't Achieve

Bill Clawson (1996) says that when he took all of the students' assessments into account, he was amazed to see their level of understanding about what their education should be. Bill believes it is necessary to read his students' papers in their entirety to see all of the ramifications of this type of self-assessment, but some of their comments give a sense of their understanding.

For example, Bill thought that Paul's response to the question, "Should students be graded on effort or accomplishment?"

would be about his own grades, since he had been very grade conscious. Paul wrote:

> I think that students should be graded on accomplishment because of one simple reason: without effort, you cannot achieve great accomplishment. A finished product will always most likely reflect and represent how much time and sweat you put into a task. The more time you put in does not mean that you will accomplish more, but the quality use of your time is what would make the difference. . . . Basketball superstar Michael Jordan is a good example of my point. With all the greatness that he has achieved, many would think that he has God-given ability for basketball, but what people do not see is the hard work and training that got him to his level. Not many people know that he was cut from his high school basketball team. . . . Nothing in life is easy, and Michael worked hard and made the team—a tribute to his effort that led to accomplishment. (Clawson 4)

Bill found another student's answer to the question, "What grade would you give yourself?" revealed a broader understanding of the effort versus accomplishment consideration. It also showed that Edward "likes things nailed down":

> I think my final grade for the project should be evaluated on the following categories: effort, class participation, how I taught the chapter, and overall effect. Each of these four categories should contribute to the final grade, and I will rate myself on a scale of 1 to 10 in each category, with 10 being the best. *Effort on the project:* The time I spent on my project was about four hours, which is a fair amount of time. My contributions to the group were just as much as my partner's or may even surpass his effort. My rating for effort would be 9.5. *Class participation:* Class participation was a definite strong point in my project mostly in part because of the charades/win, lose, or draw game. With chocolate as prizes, the class was quite cooperative and showed great enthusiasm and excitement during the game. While play-

ing the game, not a second passed by without a person in the class participating and yelling out answers. In this section, I would rate myself with a 10. *How I taught the chapter:* How I taught the chapter was important because if the summary was boring, the class would not respond, and if the questions were too easy, they would not learn anything. I tried to find a median for this dilemma and felt that my summary and questions were quite sufficient. I thought my summary could have been a little longer, but other than that, I think that I did a good job because the class did not get restless during the summary, and worked quietly, which proved that I did something right. In this portion of my grade, I would have to give myself a rating of 9. *Overall effect:* Overall effect is everything put together and probably most important. Is the presentation too fun oriented? Is it too intellectual? Is your game fun enough to get the class interested? The games were interesting and the presentation was neither too much fun, nor too intellectual. My rating in this section would be a 9. I would have to give myself a final rating of 9.5. I felt that I deserved an A. (Clawson 4–5)

I Can't Change the Entire School System

Like Bill, we were becoming uneasy with the students' dichotomy of *fun* activities and intellectual pursuits and with their sense that presentations had to involve a game with prizes. Fortunately, Bill says that another student, Sarah, came up with a "philosophical answer for the philosophical question, 'Do you think that you learn anything when you have fun (does anyone, for that matter), or does most learning come by hard work and discipline (and should that discipline come from yourself or from someone else)?' . . . Sarah wrote:

Fun vs. Discipline: Most of the *Odyssey* presentations had two parts: the part where you worked, and the part where you had fun. So which part, in my opinion, taught the class something? The answer is, it depends. I am a firm believer in "alternative" teaching methods. I think most learning should be done outside, in the field, instead of in classrooms. I don't believe in busy work and memorization. I believe people have a natural desire to learn and our school system (but not our teachers) kills that desire, until kids hate school more than anything. I not only believe learning can be fun, I believe it should be at all times. On the other hand, to learn anything worthwhile takes dedication and discipline. If it were easy to become an Olympic skier or a rocket scientist, everyone would do it. You have to work to get anything worth getting. My conclusion? Discipline has to be fun. Desirable. Students forced to memorize dates for history class will hate learning them, and forget them the second they finish taking the test. On the other hand, historians spend their lives discovering facts about the past because they want to. If you really want to achieve your goal, you will enjoy every piece of knowledge that brings you closer to it. What does all this have to do with my presentation? Nothing. I can't change the entire school system with one project. My goal was to teach students about my book of the Odyssey. I did that clearly and thoroughly, the best way I knew how. If they didn't learn anything, well, maybe they just didn't want it badly enough. (Clawson 5–6)

Sarah's response confirms what Frank Smith (1988) contends: We learn what is worthwhile, useful, and easiest to learn. Historians learn dates because they are interested in what happened then, not because it's intrinsically important to know the dates of the Civil War. Bill says that Sarah also had a surprising response to the question that asked whether students should be graded on effort or accomplishment. Sarah wrote:

Brace yourself. I'm about to make another wishy-washy, two-sided statement: I think what you should grade students on depends on the situation. In creative assignments, such as any kind of writing or art, it's important to look at effort. A student from another country who has good ideas but bad grammar should not be graded down, and a beginning violinist should not be penalized for one small squeak. As long as a student has lived up to their utmost potential, they deserve an A. In non-creative assignments, however, either you do it right or you don't. If you miss twenty-five out of twenty-seven math problems on a test, you fail. Period. If you can't do the math, you can't do it, and it doesn't matter how hard you tried. Maybe you should think about getting a tutor. (Clawson, 6)

We found Sarah's analysis interesting. However, we know many math teachers who would be willing to count effort by giving credit for "showing one's work." At the same time, we know too many arts and literature teachers who take a cut-and-dried approach to tests and assignments: Items are either right or wrong. But we understand Sarah's point, and Bill found Sarah's answer to the question of how she felt about her own grade the most interesting of all her comments. Sarah wrote:

For this particular project, I think I deserve an A–. I believe I came within a hair's breadth of living up to my potential as far as achievement goes, and I certainly tried hard. First of all, the fact is I did what was requested for the assignment. Jenny and I performed every task we were supposed to. Secondly, it has been confirmed by classmates that they learned from our project. They remembered and understood what we taught them. Thirdly, Jenny and I spent every second of free time we had working on this project. We did the best, most thorough job we could in such a short time. Fourthly, I believe the ideas we introduced to the class were good ones. The ideas of hospitality, treatment of women, reading of signs, and treatment of slaves are all important parts of the Odyssey and life in Greek times. The only fault our project has is that it wasn't fun. I believe we did our job well. We and the students benefited from our project, and due to our effort, I think we deserve an A–. (Clawson, 6)

Evaluated, Not Classified

Bill chose another student, Kimberly, as an example of how educational theory can be put into plain language. Kimberly wrote:

> Ever since I began school, my work has been evaluated and judged by a letter grade system. A letter has let me know how well I've been doing, whether I'm a "good" student or a "bad" one, and from that letter, I've been able to determine if I need to try harder, stay the same, or if I can cool it a little. I have become so dependent on this system that only because of my love of learning am I able to keep on reminding myself that what I want to accomplish is learning and creating, not an A. Students should be evaluated on what they accomplish, not graded.

As Kimberly continues, Bill says that she sounds like an addict who wants to break the habit but needs help:

> I need the letter grade to keep me in line, I use the grade as discipline and that is not where my discipline should come from. I am concerned that I would slack off and not accomplish work as good if I did not have the letter grade. What I didn't realize is that accomplishing good work is not what worries me; it is not having the security of a letter grade to tell me that I'm doing well and to tell me that I'm a good student. (Clawson 7)

Bill feels that if we'd like to revise our current educational system, we have only to ask fifteen-year-old students like Kimberly:

> When I am asked if I think grades should be based on effort or accomplishment, I would respond that students should be graded on accomplishment, but not graded with a letter. There should be feedback evaluating the weak or strong points and acknowledging the effort put into the work. Since students would be graded on the product that they produce, I believe there should

always be a way to improve, and that it should be mandatory, such as rewriting or redoing the assignment. This way the effort will count greatly but students will know that a well thought out and accomplished piece will be expected. When grades are used to determine either how much effort is put in or how accomplished a piece is, it classifies the student as either good or bad, smart or stupid. If something that was done with a lot of effort receives a bad grade and neither the effort is noticed nor a direction given for the student to follow, the student may become frustrated and more likely to give up because it is interpreted as no matter how much effort is put in, the work is still "bad." Once you're classified by a grade, it's a classification that follows you throughout life. But when you're evaluated with encouraging feedback, it is an evaluation that changes as the work improves. I keep on trying to remind myself of the purpose of school and of learning, so I can break free of the grading system I so readily depend on. (Clawson, 6–7)

With the clarity of Kimberly's words echoing in his ears, Bill has to ask,

Where is the value in all the furor about testing and assessment that goes on in public debate? If the public could depend on the most creative teachers to do the assessing, we wouldn't need the multiple-choice, high-stakes sorting out that takes place in our frenzy to "improve education." The students and the teachers, working together, could inquire into the process and see where they were. And the operative pronoun is they—teachers and students working together to learn what has to be done. And sometimes what has to be done is to make a closer relationship between the student and the teacher. This cannot be done if the grading process is a one-way street—i.e. the teacher giving points for every discrete item in the process, and the student taking it, from all sources—parents, colleges, teachers, friends, society, and sadly, even probation officers. We must put hope into the formula. I hope as we change our teaching techniques and as we look for more authentic assessment, we keep in mind that students can become better at assessing their own progress. But the big step for teachers is first understanding the value in self-assessment and then making it possible for students to do it and do it well and frequently. The idea of the portfolio is not just for teachers to assess students but for students to see their own progress and work for improvement. As Kimberly tells us, it is not worthwhile to be classified; it is worthwhile to be evaluated so that you can improve. If we work with our students and help them to see that their education is theirs and not ours, it may lead them to trust the whole educational process more, and it may lead us to trust them as thinkers and workers and not products that we turn out. (7–8)

Teacher Assessment: Listening to Students

Elizabeth Dore (1997), currently an assistant professor of education at Radford University in Virginia, speaks of an instrument she produced to help her evaluate her own performance as a public school teacher in Maine.

Each spring I developed a self-evaluation instrument whereby the students would rate the activities we had worked on during the past year. They were also free to comment on my teaching styles and my relationships within the classroom and during extracurricular activities. They knew these evaluations would not be read until school was over, and therefore, they felt free to . . . say what they truly felt. This was especially helpful to me as I planned the next school year and as I reflected on my own teaching. Sometimes this evaluation hurts and sometimes it makes me laugh, but it always makes me stop and think—Did I really do that? Is that what I wanted them to learn from that activity? In higher education, I use the same type of teacher self-evaluation instrument at the end of each semester in each and

175

every class. Again, it is most helpful when I am planning my next class. (3)

Rick Chambers (1997), before leaving his secondary classroom to take a new position at the Ontario College of Teachers, explained to his students that he would be helping teachers by working with a team of experts to establish criteria for good teaching. Rick asked them what should be on the list. The points that his students generated made Rick's last day in secondary school memorable because his students reinforced what he believed about good teaching. Rick swears that he did not coach them about what to say; he simply recorded what they said. Cynics might see what they said as a sly attempt to make teacher-pleasing remarks, but we believe their comments reflect the type of classroom they must have been in all year. Some of the comments were about what they believe a good teacher should do:

- model behavior that they want from their students—punctuality, respect, discipline, hard work, good writing, a reading habit, etc.
- understand student needs
- earn the students' respect
- encourage students to work with other students
- allow students to learn from each other
- learn with their students; there's no necessity to be the "fountain of knowledge"; students like to know that teachers don't know everything—it makes them more human
- try to find newer materials for students to study, or be open to students' suggestions
- allow students to do homework if they feel they need to do it—not assign the same work to everyone, even though some people can easily do the work, and others might struggle
- encourage students to think for themselves, to be critical thinkers, to be creative and lateral problem solvers
- avoid embarrassing any student
- demonstrate that they're interested in helping students to learn

- create the environment in which learning can comfortably take place: intimidation and negativism have no place in a learning environment
- allow students to construct their own meaning; let them make the work their own, not the teacher's interpretation alone
- allow students time to work: don't interrupt
- remember what it was like to be a student

Such simple advice: if teachers could remember what it was like to be a student—how many class periods seemed to drag on, how intimidated they felt by those who had the right answer, how meaningless they found many assignments, how vividly they remember the tasks that connected to their adolescent lives, how crucial and at the same time how absurd getting good grades was. Rick's students also had some definite ideas about assessment and evaluation; they felt good teachers should

- encourage students to take responsibility for their own learning; give away responsibility; help students grow; negotiate consequences beforehand; be positive
- differentiate between teaching and learning; a teacher's job should be to encourage learning, and to focus on how to help students learn
- assign more projects, and have fewer tests so that students can demonstrate what they know
- provide opportunities for demonstrations of learning, other than testing
- avoid asking students to memorize useless information
- validate students' ideas: allow them to be creative; allow them to make mistakes; encourage their learning through risk-taking and experimentation
- use the action research approach to learning, which emphasizes students' reflection on their learning
- avoid using Scantron tests—too much picky information, not enough opportunity for students to demonstrate what they know
- ensure that assessment is equal and fair

- use rubrics when they evaluate; negotiate rubrics with classes
- work, mark collaboratively with other teachers to ensure consistency, avoid favoritism
- make reflection a part of their curriculum: give students time to reflect on how and what they're learning
- provide positive reinforcement
- be patient, unbiased, open minded; set high but realistic standards
- set clear expectations for a class or an assignment

Some of the comments Rick's students made are quite profound; others seem obvious. What teacher doesn't have clear expectations for an assignment? There must be enough in the collective class experience for these students to mention it. Some of the other obvious qualities mentioned can give teachers chills if we consider that there must be a number of violators of these suggestions (perhaps we have been guilty at some time). Teachers should

- have no preconceived ideas about students before they meet them
- have a sense of humor and practice it
- avoid shaming or singling out students; at the same time, don't ignore them
- appear to like and respect students
- show their love for teaching through their enthusiasm every day
- make learning fun

As Bill Clawson and Rick Chambers found out, learning should be enjoyable. When did learning and having fun become mutually exclusive activities?

Thoughts for Further Inquiry

1. Informally interview parents about their children's report cards. What do they feel report cards tell them? What do

they like/dislike about report cards? What does this information tell us, as teachers?

2. Look at the content in one of the books in E. D. Hirsch Jr.'s Core Knowledge Series. How do you feel about the content in the book? How does a book like this define *cultural literacy*? Who determines what people should know? How is it determined? Who and what is left out of such definitions?

3. Discuss ways parents can be more actively involved in what goes on in your school. How can you bring your school to the community?

4. Any marketing person will tell you that public relations (PR) are important. How can you or your students be PR people for your classroom or school? Try writing to your local newspaper (individually or as a group) celebrating the learning taking place in your classroom. (Hint: Don't be defensive or negative; remember that you're writing about a positive learning experience.)

5. Discuss how grades should be determined: on progress? effort? growth? Is all learning fun? Is *fun* the same as enjoyable or satisfying?

7

Standards and Standardization

The Politics of Assessment and Evaluation

Standardized tests provide *no evidence whatsoever* that supports the myth of a recent decline in the school achievement of the average American student. Achievement in mathematics has not declined—nor has that for science, English-language competency, or any other academic subject that we know of.

—David Berliner and Bruce Biddle

There is no doubt in any teacher's mind that assessment, evaluation, grades, and test scores are politically charged. Public opinion polls continue to show taxpayers dismayed at the state of education in the country, although paradoxically they are satisfied with their local schools: Although "only 19 percent of respondents gave the nation's schools a grade of A or B . . . when *parents* were asked about the local school that served their children, a whopping 72 percent gave that school an A or B" (Berliner and Biddle 1995, 112). Newspapers and political campaigns constantly report accounts of educational decline, often based on limited evidence, and candidates running for public office see that public education found wanting makes a much better campaign issue than student and teacher success stories. The television and print media feed these perceptions because reports of positive experiences or progress in schools just doesn't provoke conversation and controversy, which raise Nielsen ratings and sell newspapers. Reporting what's good is simply not done by the media because it's not news—it doesn't have any interest or angle. Blasting teachers and schools is more headline worthy when making promises or calling for much-needed reforms (whether or not such reforms are educationally sound). "Good-hearted Americans have come to believe that the public schools of their nation are in a crisis state because they have so often been given this false message by supposedly credible sources" (Berliner and Biddle 1995, 3).

In an attack on public schools, Presidential candidate Bob Dole, in a 1996 pre-election speech to educators given at a Milwaukee Catholic school, said that "if education were a war, you'd be losing it. If it were a business, you would be driving it into bankruptcy. If it were a patient, it would be dying." One has to wonder on what data such judgments are based. If former Senator Dole had looked at the "American Education 1996 Report Card," published by the U.S. Department of Education, he would have discovered the proportion of high school graduates taking the core courses recommended in *A Nation at Risk* (1983), which consists of four years of English, three years of social studies, three years of science, and three years of math, has increased to 52 percent by 1994, up from 14 percent in 1982. In the same period, the percentage of graduates taking biology, chemistry, and physics has doubled from 18 percent to 36 percent. Students scoring a 3 or above in advanced placement (AP) courses tripled since 1982. The number of AP examinations receiving a passing score rose from 132,000 in 1982 to 476,00 in 1995.

Combined verbal and math scores on the SAT rose 17 points from 1982 to 1995, an improvement occurring at the same time as the numbers and ethnic diversity of test-takers are increasing. For another thing, more students than ever are staying in school. From 1972 to 1994, the dropout rate for students aged

16 to 24 fell from 14.6 percent to 10.5 percent. Public education is serving the public.

"The idea that American schools are now failing the nation is a Big Lie. And like all Big Lies, it has created a great deal of mischief and unhappiness for hard-working citizens and educators who deserved better from America's political leaders, industrialists, media figures, and others responsible for creating and spreading the Manufactured Crisis" (Berliner and Biddle 1995, 127). The fact is that education in the United States is not a dismal failure. It is failing some, but so is society. The ills that education faces are the ills that society must also face. According to the U.S. Census Bureau, the U.S. Department of Education, and the Children's Defense Fund, of the 52 million students enrolled in school in 1996:

- 5.2 million were labeled as handicapped
- 6.2 million were limited English–speaking students (including 2 million who were unable to speak any English)
- 2 million were latch-key children
- 1 million were abused and neglected children
- 1 million had lead poisoning
- 500,000 came from foster and institutional care
- 500,000 were homeless
- 375,000 were "crack babies" and children of hard-core drug users
- 30,000 had fetal alcohol syndrome
- one in five lived with a mother who did not finish high school
- one in five came from homes of abject poverty (including one in two who came to school hungry)

Are these excuses for delivering a poor education? No, of course not. Do we have to continue to improve our schools? Of course we do. But these statistics illustrate how difficult a job teachers have undertaken when they seek to educate *all children*—not just the "gifted" and blessed. Schools, like society, must address the needs of all children in the many cities, suburbs, and rural communities all across America. In his book *Possible Lives* (1995), Mike Rose looked at what public education is doing right, visiting schools from Los Angeles to Calexico, California, to Chicago to Tupelo and Tucson to see what made them work. What he found were enthusiastic, imaginative teachers and dedicated administrators, communities, and schools working together because they believe in kids. From this experience, Rose affirmed his belief in the promise of public education and the power of the classroom.

Media Reporting of Achievement

Our schools and our children are constantly compared to students in foreign countries, especially in the areas of math and science, and the comparisons are seldom favorable. Although these claims are unfair and inaccurate (see Berliner and Biddle 1995), they lead to the perception that our schools are in crisis. In fact, the American Education 1996 Report Card showed U.S. students scored near the top on the latest international assessment of reading. American fourth-graders outperformed students from all other nations except Finland. American fourth-graders placed third in science and above the international average in math, according to the 1997 Third International Math and Science Study. We don't place a great deal of faith in national and international comparisons; we only mention these results to argue that the hype of an education crisis sells better than a good report card.

Elliot Eisner finds

> more than a little ambivalence in our own behavior concerning test scores. We have a strong tendency to proclaim the educational poverty of test scores and then turn around and use them as indices of our own success, thus legitimating the validity of the public's concerns about the quality of education. If test scores in their conventional form do not reveal what really matters in schools, we should not use them to judge our "success." At the same time, until

we have something that is better than what we have been using, I fear we will be obliged to continue to use what we believe does not matter from an educational perspective (1992, 4)

Bad-mouthing teachers and students is hardly exclusive to American education. When we visited the United Kingdom this past summer, we weren't surprised to read in London newspapers of the poor performance of British children in the areas of reading; that is typical news reporting. The reports reminded us of home. The poorest results were in inner cities and in impoverished school districts. The schools themselves were blamed for the poor results, and of course no mention was made of the different roles literacy plays in the communities where those children live and the communities where children come from homes where parents are university educated and members of the cultural elite. Nor was any mention made of the accuracy of the measurement that led to such a conclusion.

We were surprised, however, by the reports of the university-bound students' proficient performance on their A-level exams, a positive measure of their high school performance and the key to their acceptance into a university. Of course, the news story contended that because the scores of the seniors were so high this year, many A-level students still were having difficulty finding spots at a university. The conclusion being drawn was that the high number of good grades indicated that the exams must have been easier this year. Such thinking shows that educators and students just can't win. Not one account that we read congratulated the teachers and learners on a job well done because the mindset is that students are not learning and teachers don't do a good job teaching. The public appears to expect poor test results. "Why, in this country [England], are so many suspicious of success?" asks Kathleen Tattersall (1996), chief executive of the Northern Examinations and Assessment Board. "Let us celebrate schemes of assessment that enable more young people to achieve higher standards of attainment" (28).

A newspaper reporter from a town outside Philadelphia recently asked us whether the amount of money spent per pupil in a district was indicative of student achievement, especially as reported by standardized test scores. Kathleen avoided predicting a correlation between funding and test scores, but she did tell the reporter that money isn't the only factor. Common sense will tell us that money spent on the tools of education will have an impact on the learning that takes place within a school building: money spent on staffing, resulting in smaller class size; consultants, providing support services to teachers; technology, bringing the world into the classroom; facilities, providing a positive, safe, and healthy learning environment; library books, providing not only information, but encouraging reading as a part of life.

U.S. education isn't a dismal failure; we aren't losing the war, but our schools are failing some. Assessment is not to determine who's failing and who's to blame, but to determine who's floundering and how we're going to help.

National Standards: What Are They and Who Writes Them?

In recent years, and in a large part in response to the perception that school curriculum is weak, the government has encouraged the development of standards in several content areas. In 1989 the National Council of Teachers of Mathematics published their framework for mathematics instruction K–12. The framework was built on the belief that "to learn means more than to memorize and repeat. Learning involves investigating, formulating, representing, reasoning, and using appropriate strategies to solve problems, and then reflecting on how mathematics is being used" (Romberg 1993, 36). These standards were an important part of the education summit held by the Bush administration, during which the National Governor's Association, led by then-Governor Clinton, saw the standards as an integral part of school

185

reform and a good example of what was needed. During President Clinton's first term in office, several organizations were given the task of writing standards for their disciplines.

For example, subject matter standards were released between 1994 and 1996 by these professional organizations: National Center for History in the Schools (University of California), National Council for Social Studies (Washington, D.C.), and the Center for Civic Education (Calabasas, California). Other content areas, such as the arts and the sciences, developed subject matter standards through an alliance of relevant professional organizations. For example, the science standards were drawn up by the National Academy of Science, the American Association for the Advancement of Science, the American Association of Physics Teachers, the American Chemical Society, the Council of State Science Supervisors, the Earth Science Coalition, and the National Association of Biology Teachers.

However, not all standards were met with the excitement that the math standards had generated a few years earlier. In 1992, the U.S. Department of Education awarded a grant for the Standards Project for the English Language Arts to the Center for the Study of Reading at the University of Illinois, with the agreement that NCTE and IRA would work closely with the Center. In 1994, after judging the English standards to be unsatisfactory and too general, the involvement of the Federal government ended and the International Reading Association and the National Council of Teachers of English continued to work at their own expense. The standards, published in 1996 under the title, *Standards for the English Language Arts*, have been met with both criticism and praise.

The document published by NCTE and IRA listed the twelve standards for English Language Arts (Figure 7.1). Critics of these standards maintain that they are too general, abstract, and jargon ladened. John Leo (1996), of *U.S. News and World Report*, wrote that "bad prose hides bad thinking" (61). Leo criticized the document's child centeredness and cultural relativism; others found fault without ever reading the standards. Some in the profession were harsh in their criticism because of a difference in their perception of teaching and their definition of the English language arts. Jeff Zorn (1997) of Santa Clara University in California, a critic of the standards, believes that English teachers should not "honor ignorance, illogic, and ugliness, even if it communicates perfectly to a selected audience," based on his interpretation of the standard's respect for diversity in language use, patterns, and dialects across cultures (84). Zorn's beliefs are contrary to those of others, such as James Brewbaker (1997) who teaches at Columbus State University in Georgia, who see the standards as providing direction for English teachers while providing the openness to teach in ways that are not prescriptive. Brewbaker feels that the absence of specific benchmarks in the *Standards* document are a strength and cites Louann Reid of Colorado State University, who points out that the generality of the guidelines "allows districts to set their own proficiences in ways that . . . best meet the needs of their communities" (78).

Figure 7.1   IRA/NCTE Standards for the English Language Arts

The vision guiding these standards is that all students have the opportunities and resources to develop the language skills they need to pursue life's goals and to participate fully as informed, productive members of society. These standards assume that literacy growth begins before children enter school as they experience and experiment with literacy activities—reading and writing, and associating spoken words with their graphic representations. Recognizing this fact, these standards encourage the development of curriculum and instruction that make productive use of the emerging literacy abilities that children bring to school. Furthermore, the standards provide ample room for the innovation and creativity essential to teaching and learning. They are not prescriptions for particular curriculum or instruction.

Although we present these standards as a list, we want to emphasize that they are not distinct and separable; they are, in fact, interrelated and should be considered as a whole.

1. Students read a wide range of print and nonprint texts to build an understanding of texts, of themselves, and of the cultures of the United States and the world; to acquire new information; to

respond to the needs and demands of society and the workplace; and for personal fulfillment. Among these texts are fiction and nonfiction, classic and contemporary works.

2. Students read a wide range of literature from many periods in many genres to build an understanding of the many dimensions (e.g., philosophical, ethical, aesthetic) of human experience.

3. Students apply a wide range of strategies to comprehend, interpret, evaluate, and appreciate texts. They draw on their prior experience, their interactions with other readers and writers, their knowledge of word meaning and of other texts, their word identification strategies, and their understanding of textual features (e.g., sound-letter correspondence, sentence structure, context, graphics).

4. Students adjust their use of spoken, written, and visual language (e.g., conventions, style, vocabulary) to communicate effectively with a variety of audiences and for different purposes.

5. Students employ a wide range of strategies as they write and use different writing process elements appropriately to communicate with different audiences for a variety of purposes.

6. Students apply knowledge of language structure, language conventions (e.g., spelling and punctuation), media techniques, figurative language, and genre to create, critique, and discuss print and nonprint texts.

7. Students conduct research on issues and interests by generating ideas and questions, and by posing problems. They gather, evaluate, and synthesize data from a variety of sources (e.g., print and nonprint texts, artifacts, people) to communicate their discoveries in ways that suit their purpose and audience.

8. Students use a variety of technological and informational resources (e.g., libraries, databases, computer networks, video) to gather and synthesize information and to create and communicate knowledge.

9. Students develop an understanding of and respect for diversity in language use, patterns, and dialects across cultures, ethnic groups, geographic regions, and social roles.

10. Students whose first language is not English make use of their first language to develop competency in the English language arts and to develop understanding of content across the curriculum.

11. Students participate as knowledgeable, reflective, creative, and critical members of a variety of literacy communities.

12. Students use spoken, written, and visual language to accomplish their own purposes (e.g., for learning, enjoyment, persuasion, and the exchange of information).

The *Standards* document states that these standards are intended to serve as guidelines that provide ample room for the kinds of innovation and creativity that are essential to teaching and learning. They are not meant to be seen as prescriptions for particular curricular or instructional approaches (2). In other words, these standards support teachers instead of dictating to teachers what and how they should teach. This, probably, has been the focus of most of the criticism this document has received; it looks at teachers as decision-making professionals.

It's obvious that standards are difficult to agree upon because educators, politicians, and the general public all have varied perceptions about what is important, and all have different agendas both within and outside the profession. Curriculum must look at students' interests, cultures, development, and needs. Should students in Anchorage learn the same things as children in New York City? in Miami? in St. Paul? Certainly we could agree on some generalities, but knowledge must be created in a context, and context is dependent on factors such as culture and need.

Elliot Eisner (1992) concurs:

> As a profession we are currently unable to give the public an assessment of our own schools in ways that reflect what we really care about. Our ability as a profession to assess what matters and to provide a telling picture of the strengths and weaknesses of our institution and the capabilities of our students on dimensions that have educational, not simply statistical, significance, is quite short of what we need. This shortfall has been a function, in part, of our history in testing. We have looked toward specialized agencies to provide precise, discrete, measured indicators of student performance on tests that reflect more the technical aspirations of psychometricians than the educational values of teachers. We have been part of a tradition that has not served us well, and we have not, as a profession, created alternatives. (4)

California Dreamin'

Many states are suffering from standards envy. Late in 1996, an education commission reported its progress developing California's first math and English standards that would serve as rigorous high school graduation requirements. The state's Superintendent of Public Instruction, Delaine Eastin, said the proposed requirements are necessary "to replace the 'Mickey Mouse classes' many students can now take to graduate" (Asimov 1996, A1). Superintendent Eastin went on to say, "We've never had standards in California before; [students have] to take twenty-four courses to graduate, but we only tell [them] what thirteen of [those courses] are. We say that you have to take two math classes, but if your school district says you can take Mickey Mouse classes, that's enough." The proposed standards in math and English would require one year each of algebra and geometry and the reading of "the equivalent of twenty-five books each year in a variety of genres" (Asimov 1996, A1).

One California English teacher, Carol Jago (1997), tackles the standards issue with an analogy about her son James winning a place on the state Olympic Development Soccer Team.

> I honestly did not believe he had the determination to make the state soccer team, but my son achieved what I had thought impossible. He knew how high Olympic Development Team standards were and stretched to reach them.
>
> Many, including the President, want to push young people to meet rigorous academic standards. At the top of Clinton's education agenda is a "challenge to the nation" to adopt national standards and test each fourth grader in reading and every eighth grader in math. Forty-eight of the fifty states either have standards in place or are in the process of writing them. The assumption is that setting high standards and holding students to them will improve their academic performance. . . .
>
> I am reluctant to embrace standards as the solution to

America's education ills. What worries me is that they are likely to penalize children who, through no fault of their own, attend under-staffed, poorly supported, unsafe schools. The recent expose of conditions in Compton demonstrates how children can be victimized by a system that does not have their best interest at heart. While my son James was working toward Olympic Development Team standards, he had every advantage: accomplished coaches, supportive teammates, transportation to practice and games, all the gear he needed. . . . If each child in California could be assured such ideal conditions for meeting academic standards, I would heartily support the initiative. Until that is the case, I urge caution.

President Bill Clinton and Hillary Clinton should complement their visits to high-performing suburban schools with a few in their own backyard. Washington D.C. public schools are some of the worst in the nation. New tests are not going to tell us anything the old ones haven't already about how well children in our capitol read and write. But before we blame kids for performing poorly, let's make sure they have the same chances for success that my son James and their daughter Chelsea do. (D1)

Another California resident, Edward Fry (1997), professor emeritus of education at Rutgers University and a former adviser to the National Assessment of Educational Progress, in an open letter to the president took issue with his standards.

Standards work pretty well in math, or spelling, or geography, where a finite body of knowledge can be specified. Can a student correctly add three four-digit numbers? Can he or she correctly spell the one thousand most common words by the end of the fourth grade? Can a student fill in a map naming all fifty states? But when it comes to reading, setting standards is more formidable. For example, can a fourth grader read a story like "Peter Rabbit" and understand it? Well, what do we mean by "understand"? What's the main idea of "Peter Rabbit"? (not a very sensible question). Is the story of Peter Rabbit an allegory?

(not too good for fourth grade). Does Mr. MacGregor like Peter? (a little simplistic). Well, you get the idea. . . .

There is another very basic idea you must grasp, and that is that most human abilities follow a normal distribution curve. This means that any group of children or adults have different amounts of most any ability; the ability to throw a basketball accurately, to play the saxophone, to grasp mathematical concepts, or to "read.". . . Incidentally, you and Secretary of Education Richard W. Riley sometimes publicly state the head-line-grabbing statistic that some 44 percent of fourth graders don't even come up to a "basic reading level." Let me point out that a "basic level" is merely the subjective opinion of some unnamed group of "experts." It is sort of a "wouldn't it be nice if they could" basic level of achievement. It is not a condemnation of public education that a large group of students can't do what some experts just thought up as a new "basic standard." (2–3)

California's Nightmare

Assessments continue to be politically volatile. Sometimes when educators and politicians seem to be going in the right direction, the public's misconceptions and distrust stop the wheels in motion and sometimes begin to roll back to what is familiar and comfortable—the "old ways are the best ways" mentality. Such was the case with the short-lived California Learning Assessment System (CLAS) implemented in 1993 and abandoned soon after. "For a variety of reasons, . . . parents, conservative religious groups, the California Boards Association, the California Teachers Association (CTA), and the governor all raised objections to the assessment during its 1993 implementation" (Kirst and Mazzeo 1996, 319).

It's important to review what happened to CLAS because its history illustrates some of the problems that districts and states will continually face as they try to reform or update traditional behavioral testing procedures.

The goals of CLAS seemed simple enough, but in and of

themselves they were politically loaded. They included the goals:

1. "To align California's testing system to the content of what was taught in schools, as represented in state curricular frameworks;
2. To better measure attainment of curricular content through *performance-based* standards and assessment; and
3. To provide assessment of individual student performance as well as data on schools and districts" (Kirst and Mazzeo 1996, 320).

The tests would be given once a year and would be combined with portfolios to keep track of student work over a longer period of time.

Rumors circulated almost immediately about "objectionable content" on these tests. The rumors, fed by conservative religious groups, were fueled by the California Department of Education's decision to secure test questions so they could be used more than once. Without the questions being made public, people could claim just about anything. This lack of communication did nothing to dispel rumors that the test questions undermined parents' right to teach moral values to their children and invaded the privacy of students and their families. Others objected to the choice of reading selections. By the end of 1993, three texts had been removed as reading prompts for the test: "Roselily" and "Am I Blue" by Alice Walker, and an excerpt from *An American Childhood* by Annie Dillard. "Roselily" was pulled because of pressure from "the Traditional Values Coalition, a conservative Christian group, who called the story *anti-religious* because of the phrase, 'the wrong God,' and the sentence, 'She thinks of ropes, chains, handcuffs, his religion'" (Dudley 1997, 18). The second Walker reading, "Am I Blue," was "removed from the test because two members of the California Board of Education felt that tenth-grade students might be so upset over the death of the horse in the story that they would be unable to do their best on the test and also because it was *anti-meat-eating*" (18). And the Dillard piece was cut because members of the board "considered the story *too violent* because it recounts a snowball-throwing episode from the author's childhood" (18).

Figure 7.2   Sample Reading Test

(version of a CLAS test developed by Sheridan Blau (1998) to show the features of the test in an abbreviated form)

Read the poem that appears below and answer the questions that follow. Feel free to make notes in the margin as you read.

Introductory Note: This poem by Emma Lazarus (1849–1887) was selected in 1886 to be inscribed on the pedestal of the Statue of Liberty, which stands in New York Harbor (between New York City and Jersey City, New Jersey) at the entrance to the Port of New York. Every boat entering the Port of New York passes within view of the statue. For generations New York was the port of arrival for most immigrants entering the U.S. by boat, so that for most immigrants the Statue of Liberty was the symbol of welcome to the U.S. The original "Colossus," one of the seven wonders of the ancient world, was a huge statue that straddled the harbor of Rhodes in ancient Greece.

The New Colossus (1883)   *Your Notes*
Not like the brazen giant of Greek fame,
With conquering limbs astride from land to land;
Here at our sea-washed, sunset gates shall stand
A mighty woman with a torch, whose flame
Is the imprisoned lightning, and her name
Mother of Exiles. From her beacon-hand
Glows world-wide welcome; her mild eyes command
The air-bridged harbor that twin cities frame.
"Keep, ancient lands, your storied pomp!" cries she
With silent lips. "Give me your tired, your poor,
Your huddled masses yearning to breathe free,
The wretched refuse of your teeming shore.
Send these, the homeless, tempest-tossed to me,
I lift my lamp beside the golden door!"

1. What is your initial reaction or response (your thoughts, feelings, observations, questions, ideas, etc.) to this poem?

2. Pick a line in this poem that seems to you especially important or interesting. Write out the line and then explain your reasons for selecting it.

3. How do you interpret the name "Mother of Exiles" in line 6? What is the significance of this name in the poem?

4. The last part of the poem says, "Give *me your* tired, *your* poor."
   a. Who is "me" and who is you or "your?" Who is speaking in the last five lines of this poem and to whom are these lines addressed?

   b. Using the "Open Mind" outline provided [on full page in actual test], show with drawings, symbols, or words what the speaker of these lines is thinking or what a person hearing these lines might be expected to think.

   c. Explain your graphic.

5. Use the opportunity provided by this question to say anything else you might want to say about this poem. You might want to talk about its form or language, its meaning to you personally or as a member of a group, its cultural or historical or ideological or aesthetic significance, or anything else you haven't already said about the poem.

Blau, Sheridan. 1998. "Politics and the English Language Arts." In *Progressive Language Policies and Practices: What Can We Learn from Particular Cases?*, edited by Carol Edelsky and Curtis Dudley-Marling. Urbana, IL: NCTE.

Teachers who had worked on the development of this test were furious that a handful of citizens would be successful at censoring reading selections that were of literary merit and valuable prompts for assessing students' literacy development. The CLAS test questions (Figure 7.2), rather than being one-answer, multiple-choice questions, require the reader to respond using thoughts, feelings, observations, questions, ideas, etc., employing a reader response approach to the text (Rosenblatt 1978) rather than a strictly analytical approach. The questions provide students with an opportunity to use language to communicate thought and perception. Scoring these tests required readers who were trained in holistic scoring using anchor papers and a 1–6 rubric (Figure 7.3). Obviously this type of performance is different from an "objective" Scantron type of test. Not understanding the reasons and possibilities for such testing, the public and even some educators were worried about validity and reliability.

Figure 7.3 Scoring Rubric for the CLAS Reading Test, California Department of Education, Sacramento, CA, 1994

Reading Performances
The following list of reading performances shows the range of behaviors that readers may engage in as they construct meaning from a text. Readers are not expected to exhibit all of these behaviors, but more effective readers are likely to exhibit a wider range of behaviors. In general, readers also demonstrate more advanced levels of achievement by the degree to which they attend to increasingly more complex structures of meaning.

As readers demonstrate the quality, range, and comprehensiveness of their transactions with texts through their writing and graphic representations, they:

- Demonstrate intellectual engagement with the text: experiment with ideas; think divergently; take risks; express opinions; speculate, hypothesize, visualize characters or scenes, explore alternative scenarios; raise questions; make predictions; think metaphorically
- Explore multiple possibilities of meaning; consider cultural and/or psychological nuances and complexities in text
- Fill in gaps; use clues and evidence in the passage to draw conclusions; make warranted and plausible interpretations of ideas, facts, concepts, and/or arguments

- Recognize and deal with ambiguities in the text
- Revise, reshape, and/or deepen early interpretations
- Evaluate; examine the degree of fit between the author's ideas or information and the reader's prior knowledge or experience
- Challenge and reflect critically on the text by agreeing or disagreeing, arguing, endorsing, questioning, and/or wondering
- Demonstrate understanding of the work as a whole
- Attend to the structure of the text: show how the parts work together; how characters and/or other elements of the work are related and change
- Show aesthetic appreciation of the text; consider linguistic and structural complexities
- Allude to and/or retell specific passage(s) to validate and/or expand ideas
- Make meaning of parts of the text
- Make connections between the text and their own ideas, experiences, and knowledge
- Demonstrate emotional engagement with the text
- Retell, summarize, and/or paraphrase with purpose
- Reflect on the meaning(s) of the text, including larger or more universal significances; express a new understanding or insight

Score Point 6—Exemplary Reading Performance

An exemplary reading performance is insightful, discerning, and perceptive as the reader constructs and reflects on meaning in a text. Readers at this level are sensitive to linguistic, structural, cultural, and psychological nuances and complexities. They fill in gaps in a text, making warranted and responsible assumptions about unstated causes or motivations, or drawing meaning from subtle cues. They differentiate between literal and figurative meanings. They recognize real or seeming contradictions, exploring possibilities for their resolution or tolerating ambiguities. They demonstrate their understanding of the whole work as well as an awareness of how the parts work together to create the whole.

Readers achieving score point six develop connections with and among texts. They connect their understanding of the text not only to their own ideas, experience, and knowledge, but to their history as participants in a culture or larger community, often making connections to other texts or other works of art. Exceptional readers draw on evidence from the text to generate, validate, expand, and reflect on their own ideas.

These readers take risks. They entertain challenging ideas and explore multiple possibilities of meaning as they read, grounding

197

these meanings in their acute perceptions of textual and cultural complexities. They often revise their understanding of a text as they reread and as additional information or insight becomes available to them. They sometimes articulate a newly developed level of understanding.

Readers performing at level six challenge the text. They carry on dialogue with the writer, raising questions, taking exception, agreeing or disagreeing, appreciating or criticizing text features. They may sometimes suggest ways of rewriting the text. They may test the validity of the author's ideas or information, by considering the authority of the author and the nature and quality of evidence presented. They may speculate about the ideology or cultural or historical biases that seem to inform a text, sometimes recognizing and embracing and sometimes resisting the position a text seems to construct for its reader.

Score Point 5—Discerning Reading Performance

A reading performance at score point five is discerning, thorough, and perceptive, but will probably show somewhat less insight or sensitivity to textual nuances and complexities than exemplary reading. These readers are able to fill in gaps in a text, making plausible assumptions from subtle cues; but they engage in these operations with less acuteness of vision than more expert readers. They recognize and differentiate between literal and figurative meanings. They recognize real or seeming contradictions, exploring possibilities for their resolution or tolerating ambiguities. They demonstrate their understanding of the whole work as well as an awareness of how the parts work together to create the whole.

Readers achieving score point five see connections between their own lives and the world of the text. They connect their understanding of the text not only to their own ideas, experiences, and knowledge, but to their history as participants in a culture or community. They often make connections to other texts or other works of art; these connections, while always purposeful and connected to the text, may be more predictable than those made by exceptional readers. They also draw on evidence from the text to generate, validate, expand, and reflect on their own ideas.

These readers may explore multiple possibilities of meaning. While they may form firm interpretations early in their reading, they are open to revising their ideas as additional information or insight becomes available to them. They sometimes articulate a newly developed level of understanding.

Readers performing at this level challenge the text. They pose questions, postulate answers, take exception, agree, disagree, speculate; however, the questions and/or issues they raise may not be as insightful or perceptive as those of the reader demonstrating an exemplary reading.

Score Point 4—Thoughtful Reading Performance

Readers at score point four construct a thoughtful and plausible interpretation of a text. They fill in some gaps in a text, making assumptions about unstated causes or motivations or drawing meaning from cues in the text. They usually differentiate between literal and figurative meanings. They may recognize real or seeming contradictions, but are sometimes distracted by these contradictions and by ambiguities. They demonstrate a thoughtful understanding of the whole work.

Readers achieving score point four develop connections with and among texts. They usually connect their understanding of the text to their own experience and knowledge and sometimes to other texts. When directed, these readers may generate, validate, expand, and/or reflect on their ideas about the text, but with less depth than in a score point five or six response. These readers tend to paraphrase or retell, often thoroughly and purposefully. They also see, however, a more general significance

in or wider application of the literal facts of the text.

These readers, while confident, rarely take risks. They accept the text without exploring multiple possibilities of meaning. They tend to present their understanding of a text as fixed and rarely revise their interpretation as they reread and as additional information becomes available.

Readers demonstrating this level of reading performance sometimes challenge or question the text. They may raise questions and may agree or disagree without explaining their reactions.

Score Point 3—Literal Reading Performance

Students performing at score point three are literal readers, constructing a plausible but superficial interpretation of the whole work. They show little sensitivity to nuances and complexities; they may not respond to some portion of the text. They usually demonstrate a sense of the whole work, but at a simplistic and literal level.

These readers develop few or no connections with or among texts. Sometimes they connect the text associationally with personal experience, but the connection is generally superficial and unexamined.

These readers are not risk takers. They show little tolerance for textual difficulties or lack of closure. Confronted by textual complexity, they may not address the difficulties. Their reading process tends not to be recursive: Having made some initial sense of the text, they are inclined to retain their view without testing or revising it.

Readers at the score point three level of reading performance rarely challenge the text or carry on an internal dialogue with the writer. If they raise questions at all the questions will be largely unproductive expressions of frustration or low level inquiries (e.g., about word meanings). Any expressed appreciations or criticisms are likely to be simplistic and based on a literal understanding of the text.

Score Point 2—Limited Reading Performance

A limited reading performance indicates that readers at score point two construct partial and/or reductive meanings for a text. They may demonstrate a superficial understanding of parts of the text. They demonstrate a reductive meaning for the text by overgeneralizing or oversimplifying but seem unable to grasp the whole.

Readers within this range of performance develop few or no connections with texts. They may, as they recognize some idea, continue to write or draw, but their responses will appear to have only a tangential relevance to the text.

These readers seldom ask questions of a text or offer meaningful evaluations of what they read. They tend to abandon or become entangled in difficult sections of a text.

Score Point 1—Minimal Reading Performance

In a minimal reading performance, the reader appears to understand and respond to an individual word, title, and/or phrase but not in ways that demonstrate even a rudimentary understanding of how these words relate to text ideas.

Any connection such readers may make to their own experience will appear in the form of words or drawings that have textual associations only to an isolated word or phrase. Minimal responses may include vague and unsupported evaluations or responses (e.g., "I like/don't like this story," or "It's boring.")

Level one reader responses suggest that these students do not engage in reading as a process of making coherent meaning.

In addition to public misconceptions, CLAS was compromised by its inability to satisfy all three of its major purposes for the administration of the test in the first place, purposes for which the test was ultimately inappropriate. California Governor Pete Wilson's top priority for using the testing program was to allow for stringent accountability for teachers. California State Senator Gary Hart was interested in school performance accountability and the then–state school superintendent, Bill Honig, along with the state education department, was committed to performance-based testing and tying assessment to the curricular frameworks (Kirst and Mazzeo 1996). What is obvious from the example of CLAS is that testing is political insofar as states must first decide what they are trying to assess. Should students be tested to determine if schools are doing their jobs? Are assessments primarily for teachers so they can support students' learning? Should states use assessments to reward or punish schools, teachers, and/or students for perceived accomplishments or failures?

Sheridan Blau (1997) points out that

> while the CLAS reading test was first developed to be part of a statewide program to assess instruction (through matrix sampling) rather than individual students, the [California] Department of Education had drafted a plan to produce individual scores . . . based on a battery of tests that was to include portfolios. In all, it was a grand but probably unrealistic scheme for a testing program that would be closely connected to genuine instructional goals and hardly distinguishable from instruction itself. That is hardly a viable model for a statewide test, which . . . is more of a political than an educational instrument.

As far as CLAS is concerned, "California has been without a statewide achievement test since 1994, when Governor Pete Wilson vetoed the CLAS test after a year of fierce debate about it proved how political reading, writing, and arithmetic really are. . . . Any new state exam would be matched to the standards, [Superintendent of Public Instruction] Eastin said, so that students would have a clearer idea of what is expected of them" (Asimov 1996, A1). To add insult to injury, Governor Wilson had stipulated that teacher involvement will not be a part of any new assessment developed or implemented in the state. Fortunately, California teachers have a clearer sense of what authentic assessment is all about. Many of them still use the CLAS handbooks, scoring guides, and illustrative essays in their classrooms, maintaining that this instrument helps them assess their students' reading and writing abilities and progress and helps them articulate their expectations more effectively.

The difficulty with statewide assessments is that the parties involved (politicians, taxpayers, school board members, teachers, and parents) all have different agendas. (We know better than to include students since their voices don't seem to count in this debate.) Often students are used to satisfy political agendas and their personal learning and educational goals are of little consequence in the larger scheme of things.

Does Having Standards Mean Standardization?

Testing, usually thought to be an objective measurement of knowledge, has traditionally been used in both assessment and evaluation. Since colonial days, there has been a tacit understanding that learning in public schools needs to be monitored by testing and teachers are the ones charged with the responsibility for periodically checking the academic performance of their students. This check of performance has been accomplished by quantitatively measuring students' knowledge of facts and skills as prescribed by the curriculum. However, there has been little agreement concerning the types of tests to be used to assess student learning. Thorndike's statistical work in the early 1900s and the growth of the "testing movement in education" prompted standardized tests in arithmetic and handwriting (Micheels and Karnes 1950). By 1928, over 1,300 tests were published, and by 1944, over 60 million standardized tests were given to over 20 million people (Harp 1994).

Since research studies have shown that grading on teacher-constructed tests is very subjective, most people would believe that it is preferable to use tests that ask a large number of questions whose answers can be standardized. Although they vary in scope and purpose, standardized tests fall into two categories: norm referenced and criterion referenced. The purpose of norm-referenced tests is to measure the standing of the test-taker within some known group, such as all twelfth-graders in the United States (Gronlund 1985). Norms for the test—reference points for standards of achievement—have been derived from the average scores of a large sample of people who represent the group being measured. Consequently, scores are reported in percentiles placing the test-taker in relation to the larger sample group. For example, after taking a norm-referenced test for mathematics in tenth grade, a student might receive a score of 69, which would indicate that he or she did better than 69 percent of all students taking that test, and that 30 percent scored higher than he or she did, based on norms determined by the representative group.

Criterion-referenced tests try to provide a measure of performance based on much narrower, more clearly defined criteria. The tests are intended to indicate areas of strength and weakness, measured against a predetermined level of acceptable performance. For example, students in tenth grade might be expected to answer twenty out of thirty questions on a tenth-grade mathematics exam and if they do, a level of acceptable performance would have been reached for that grade. Both norm-referenced and criterion-referenced tests use the same types of questions, and both interpret the results according to inferential statistics. They are also both judged by the same standards of validity and reliability.

But even those two types of tests are not that clear cut. According to the NCTE/IRA Joint Task Force on Assessment (1996),

Assessment terms change as different groups appropriate them for different purposes, and as situations change. . . . For example, the term *norm-referenced* once meant that assessment data on one student, typically test data, were interpreted in comparison with the data of other students who were considered similar. . . . *Criterion-referenced* assessment once meant simply that a student's performance was interpreted with respect to a particular level of performance; either it met the criterion or it did not. Recently, however, it has become much less clear in which ways these terms are being used. The line between criterion and norm has broken down. For example, criterion has recently come to mean dimension or valued characteristic. Norm has come to be used in much the same sense. But even in the earlier (and still more common) meaning, most criteria for criterion-related tests are arrived at by finding out how a group of students performs on the test, and then setting criteria in accord with what seems a reasonable point for a student's passing or failing the test. (5)

Since Horace Mann suggested the use of standardized tests in 1845, these tests are ubiquitous for any school district. By 1878, the New York State Board of Regents instituted a statewide set of examinations. The College Board Entrance Examination for college-bound students has been around since 1900 and is still in place. In fact, for more than one hundred years, students in American schools have been subjected to tests of achievement and knowledge from kindergarten through postsecondary school for a variety of purposes, ranging from tracking to determining such things as a school's eligibility for federal and state funding and a student's admission to university and graduate programs.

A look at the testing line-up from one of our neighboring school districts shows the regimen: the Iowa Test of Basic Skills is given in every grade, from first to eighth. A Cognitive Abilities test is given in third, fifth, and seventh grade. The State Assessment Test for Math and Reading begins in fifth grade, and is given in eighth and eleventh grades. The State Assessment Test for Writing is given in sixth grade and is repeated in ninth grade. The Algebra Aptitude test is given in seventh and eighth grades. The PSAT begins to be offered in ninth grade through eleventh grade, when the National Merit Scholarship candidates take the test. Tests of Achievement and Proficiency are given in the ninth and eleventh grades. A military aptitude test, the ASVAB, is also offered in the eleventh and twelfth grades. College entrance exams, the SAT and the ACT, are offered monthly throughout the eleventh and twelfth grades. This school district could certainly be said to be fulfilling its duty of making its students test ready. A certain percentage of its students could also be said to be test defeated by the time they confront the SATs.

Problems with Standardized Testing

Education majors are often required to take a course in "tests and measurements," in which they examine clinically the virtues and drawbacks of various test designs. Preservice teachers are led to believe that a good test can be designed, if they pay attention to the level of difficulty of the questions, their type, and their content, and figure what a good result would be, in terms of number right and percentage of test-takers achieving that level. So is it not unreasonable to wonder what is being asked on these tests? One would assume the tests ask what the commissions and committees have determined are the relevant facts and skills for the individual content areas. But the relevant facts and skills that appear on the tests become the curriculum for the test-conscious teachers. Because of the significance of test results and the immense pressure they exert, teachers too often find themselves teaching to the test, in order that their students do well and the teachers appear to be doing their jobs. It works as an example of another self-fulfilling prophecy or a Slappy Hooper "skyhook," as Ken Goodman (1997) describes it:

"Years ago I had a colleague who was studying grade placement of science concepts in courses of study and text books. The text publishers said they read all the courses of study and made their decisions based on those. And the curriculum committees said they looked at all the text series and . . . you get the idea. There's a circle without substance in all that. What Slappy Hooper called a skyhook" (1).

In fact, almost since their inception, standardized tests have been met with criticism. A major problem with standardized testing is how the test results are used. Standardized tests are frequently found to be poor indicators of higher-level thinking skills and are sometimes undemocratic and even racist in their bias. Many feel that such tests are not only used incorrectly, but they are unfair to certain groups of people, since the tests are designed for a "general" population and usually ignore minority or underrepresented groups. Test results affect each student's academic life, sometimes to such a great extent that test results operationally prevent a student from being admitted to college or test results place a student within a group or track that limits the options of study and the levels of academic challenge.

Bernard Gifford, chairman of the National Commission on Testing and Public Policy, quoted in the report, "From Gatekeeper to Gateway: Transforming Testing in America," holds that "there is ample evidence that the testing enterprise has in many instances gone haywire and is driving our educational system in the wrong direction. . . . Current testing, predominantly multiple choice in format, is over-relied on, lacks adequate public accountability, sometimes leads to unfairness in the allocation of opportunities, and too often undermines social policies" (Evangelauf 1990, A1).

What most students, parents, and even teachers don't realize is that the SATs are not achievement tests. They were never designed to be. In fact, ETS warns schools not to use results to compare districts (which they must know happens regardless). School districts, fueled by the media, use SAT results to demonstrate the effectiveness of their teaching despite the fact that the test correlates strongly with socioeconomic status. The reality is that the SAT was originally developed as an aptitude test to identify students in typically rural and urban areas who had potential but were in schools that typically did not produce "college-bound" students. A vast majority of tests on the market, typically those used in special education, have been found to be unacceptable by experts in the psychometric field (Hammill, Brown, and Bryant 1989; Hall 1985). The fact is that the testing industry is big business in the United States. Despite the flaws of standardized testing, the public and the system itself have certainly bought into them (both literally and figuratively). The amount of money spent on tests is a staggering amount, paid for by taxpayers and parents. Parents pay for SAT preparatory classes and even remedial classes to try to raise their children's score. The test is impossible to study for, but such courses help students become "test-wise," to know how to answer and read tricky questions, and hopefully raise their score due to their familiarity with the test and its procedures.

When the number of test items are combined on standardized tests, program-based tests, and teacher-made tests, most students in our country are faced with two thousand test items per year (Tierney, Carter, and Desai 1991). Today, the SAT tests help transform normal students into stressed-out adolescents who push themselves academically, as sixteen-year-old Elizabeth Shaw (1997) confesses, for one reason: "acceptance to a *good* college." Shaw says that the "pressure to attend a prestigious university comes from everywhere," but specifically from "school administrators, guidance counselors, and parents" (22). She and her friends find themselves "enrolled [by their parents] in classes to raise their SAT scores a few more points" and exhausted trying "to live up to impossible levels of perfection in order to appease the unseen gods in the college admission offices" (22).

And the games don't stop at high school. At many universities, applicants for graduate programs must supply proof ("official," of course) of scores from the Graduate Record Exam (GRE), again administered by ETS at an approximate cost of one hundred dollars per student. For a long time, we resisted this requirement at our university, looking instead at applicants' grades and performance at the undergraduate level as a determinant of admittance into our programs. However, Middle States, an outside accrediting agency that evaluates most college and university programs, felt that our admissions standards lacked rigor because of the absence of an entrance exam requirement: the GRE. Students must now take the exam and pass with a certain score to be unconditionally accepted. We have to admit that to this point students haven't been denied admittance to any program because of low test grades (the test being only one criterion for admittance), but the GRE has also done nothing to help the university in selection. Past performance in academic programs is still the best predictor of success in our programs.

Many in education are calling for changes in testing. As schools and educators look at the ways they teach and how students learn, a different view of assessment and evaluation is now being called for, one that reflects a transactional philosophy. Meaningful assessment and useful evaluation methods are being employed in many classrooms and schools, and many state departments of education are recognizing the need for more appropriate measures of student performance.

All Philosophies Are Really Autobiographies

In this book about authentic assessment, what can be said about standardized tests? In his book *Beyond Good and Evil,* Nietzsche maintained that all philosophies are really autobiographies. All of us know the power of testing from our own experiences as learners and as teachers. Most teachers hate tests, finding them an interruption in the process of teaching and learning. Most tests tell teachers little about what students know. Instead, they are powerful political tools that are not about to go away.

When we reflect on our life experiences with assessments, especially with standardized tests and their effect on our lives, both personally and to a lesser extent professionally, we realize these tests have much to do with our personalities but not what the test-makers think they do.

Jim had always been a good test-taker and actually enjoyed the aptitude-type tests because they were similar to mental puzzles. He never got near-1600s like his nephews, but he didn't embarrass himself. He still enjoys Jeopardy and Trivial Pursuit games. He remembers the SATs as a chance to compete with Tom, his best friend since grade school. They got almost identical scores and both qualified for New York Regents' scholarships. One embarrassing moment came when Jim received mediocre scores in the National Merit Scholarship exam. He remembers dozing off during parts of the test because of lack of sleep. Attempts to explain away the bad scores just looked like excuse making—test results don't lie.

Kathleen was also a "good" student—decent grades, well behaved, a teacher pleaser—but high school was neither particularly interesting nor enjoyable. She was always concerned about keeping up her grades so she could be assured of getting into college and perhaps getting a scholarship. She dreaded the SATs for two years before taking them, aware of the high stakes and the one-shot experience of taking them. She also knew she couldn't prepare for the SAT, although she, like her other college-bound friends, tried to memorize lists of vocabulary words (never mind that she had been a voracious reader for eleven years). She still remembers taking this test: hundreds of her classmates in the high school gymnasium, sitting in row upon row of desks, sealing their future fates during those few hours. Kathleen was physically ill from stress before entering the gym, and the test was terrible. Her fears were realized several weeks later when her guidance counselor called her to his office and broke the news. Her scores were okay, but he was really disappointed and had expected more from her. She felt as if everyone knew what she had always secretly believed: She wasn't very smart. Nevertheless, she did get into college and received a master's and Ph.D. She is still, however, haunted by the message that test gave to her: She was a disappointment.

We know our experience is common, which makes this issue more disturbing. We've watched our children struggle with standardized tests, seeing firsthand how little the tests tell educators, parents, and students themselves about anything, especially learning. We've also been witness to their power. Our daughter Laura took the SATs twice, scoring lower the second time, yet she graduated from college *summa cum laude*. When she felt humiliated and hurt after receiving her SAT scores, we reminded her these tests were not her forte (even in elementary school her test scores were lower than her performance so her teachers labelled her an "over-achiever"). Understandably, when it was time to take the GRE, she approached it with the same defeatist attitude (nevertheless, she was accepted into graduate studies and has a 4.0 QPA so far). Laura had learned a lesson from these exams: These tests convinced her that the grades she received were "luck" and the scores on the test were a more accurate assessment of her abilities.

Many educators understand the problems, implications, and politics of the standardized test craze in this country, but we usually complain amongst ourselves—preaching to the choir. However, our voices as educators must work to educate those outside our field (and sometimes within our field), and help people understand that standardized tests cannot do what most think they can: They cannot make education better, nor can they help schools or students. In the meantime, the only thing we can do is to try to keep standardized tests in perspective. We must not let them control our curriculum nor our teaching, and we must be advocates for our students as they continue to be subjected to these tests and the consequences of test scores.

Accountability

Although we've made it clear throughout this book that we feel that assessment and evaluation are ways to support learning, we have said little about why assessment and evaluation should be used to take a look at how we're doing as teachers. Some teachers, such as Rick Chambers and Jim Mahoney, use their students' portfolios as a way to self-assess and others, like Maureen Neal and Jane Blystone, use written dialogue and conferences to gauge their success. John Dewey (1983) said, "We make a religion out of education, we profess unbounded faith in its possibilities. . . . But on the other hand, we assume in practice that no one is specifically responsible when bad outcomes show themselves. . . . When results are undesirable, we shrug our shoulders and place the responsibility upon some intrinsic defect or outer chance" (126). It's easy to take credit for what's right in education, but we also have to look at how we are "failing" and take responsibility to make education better for all students. We know that there are problems, that kids come to school with baggage, and that education often has to compete with television, outside jobs, family problems, and pressures of one kind or another, including adolescent problems. These can't be excuses for not learning; they are things we deal with in school as we work to make school learning real enough to find a place in today's world.

Assessment and evaluation that are authentic should make us more accountable. Like naturalistic researchers, our job is to look for evidence from a variety of sources, piece it together to make sense of what is happening, and use this information to support our decisions for the sake of student learning. We are the professionals and we are responsible for making this happen—for all kids, in all schools. That is the promise and the hope of education.

Thoughts for Further Inquiry

1. In the library, search newspapers and popular news journals (e.g., *Newsweek*, *Time*, *U.S. News and World Report*) for stories about education (especially ones that deal with results). How are the stories reported? Were there any responses to the stories the following week, especially from educators?
2. In your school district, or one that is accessible, find out how many tests are given to students in grades K–12. What are

211

these tests used for? Do they support student learning or help teachers in any ways?

3. Read about successful schools in Mike Rose's *Possible Lives* (1995). Are there common denominators for success?
4. Take the CLAS reading test (Figure 7.2). After answering these test questions, discuss with others in your group your answers as well as your experience taking this test. Look at the scoring rubric (Figure 7.3) and discuss if this test could be a help to students and/or teachers.
5. Discuss the role standardized testing has played in your life as a learner or as a teacher.

References

Asimov, N. 1996. "Graduation Standards Proposed: State Raises Level to Finish High School." *San Francisco Chronicle*, 13 November, A1.

Atwell, N. 1987. *In the Middle: Writing, Reading, and Learning with Adolescents*. Portsmouth, NH: Boynton/Cook.

Baker, C. 1996. "Dear Reader Essay." Hempfield Area High School, PA.

Bellanca, J. A., and R. Fogarty. 1991. *Blueprints for Thinking in the Cooperative Classroom*. 2nd ed. Palatine, IL: IRI/Skylight Publishing.

Berge, C. 1997. Reaching Out to Parents. Paper presented at annual meeting of National Council of Teachers of English, Charlotte, NC, April 10–12.

Berliner, D. C., and B. J. Biddle. 1995. *The Manufactured Crisis: Myths, Fraud, and the Attack on America's Public Schools*. Reading, MA: Addison-Wesley.

Blau, S. 1997. Personal correspondence, September 11.

———. 1998. "Politics and the English Language Arts." In *Progressive Language Policies and Practices: What Can We Learn from Particular Cases?*, edited by Carol Edelsky and Curtis Dudley-Marling. Urbana, IL: National Council of Teachers of English.

Bloom. B., G. Madaus, and J. Hastings. 1981. *Evaluation to Improve Learning*. New York: McGraw-Hill.

Blystone, J. 1997a. E-mail correspondence, January 5.

———. 1997b. E-mail correspondence, January 22.

———. 1997c. E-mail correspondence, October 31.

Brewbaker, J. 1997. "On Tuesday Morning: The Case for Standards for the English Language Arts." *English Journal* 86 (1): 76–82.

Broughton, E. 1997. Personal correspondence, January 3.

Burke, J. 1996. "The Measure of Our Success." Unpublished manuscript.

Butler, K. 1996. "My Views on Assessment." Hempfield Area High School, PA.

Chambers, R. 1993. "Integrating Personal and Literary Response." *English Leadership Quarterly* 15 (4): 7–8.

———. 1996. Portfolio Writing and Learning: An Action Research Project. Unpublished manuscript.

———. 1997. Personal correspondence, May 6.

Clawson, B. 1996. E-mail correspondence, October 26. Revision of "Self-Assessment as Authentic Assessment." Originally published in *CLIPs: A Journal of the California Literature Project*, Summer 1994. University of California, San Diego.

Clay, M. 1990. "Research Current: What Is and What Might Be Evaluation." *Language Arts* 67 (3): 288–298.

Clinton, President W. J. 1997, February 4. "State of the Union Address." http://library.whitehouse.gov/

Collins, A., and D. Genter. 1989. Cited in "A Systematic Approach to Educational Testing" by J. R. Fredirksen and Allan Collins. *Educational Researcher* (December): 27–32.

Conger, J. 1997. "Journalistic Writing Semester Exam." Downer's Grove High School, Downer's Grove, IL.

Cowden, J. 1996. Portfolio Directions Handout. Big Spring High School, Newville, PA.

Crouse, J. S. 1996. "Dear Reader Essay." Hempfield Area High School, PA.

Dandoy, B. 1996. Personal interview. Karns City Area High School, PA, October 15.

Davidson, D. M. 1993. *The Cereal Murders*. New York: Bantam.

Dewey, J. 1983. "Education as Religion." In *The Middle Works of John Dewey: 1899–1924*, edited by J. A. Boydston. Carbondale: Southern Illinois University Press.

DiMarco, D. 1997. E-mail correspondence, June 25.

Dore, E. 1997. Assessment and Evaluation. Unpublished manuscript.

Dreyer, D. 1994. "When Models Collide." *English Leadership Quarterly* 16 (1): 9–11.

Dudley, M. 1997. "The Rise and Fall of a Statewide Assessment System." *English Journal* 86 (1): 15–20.

Eisner, E. 1992. "The Reality of Reform." *English Leadership Quarterly* 14 (3): 2–5.

Evangelauf, J. 1990. "Reliance on Multiple-choice Tests Said to Harm Minorities and Hinder Reform; Panel Seeks a New Regulatory Agency." *The Chronicle of Higher Education* 37, A1.

Fleischer, C. 1997. Taking It to the Streets: Teachers as Advocates. Paper presented at annual meeting of National Council of Teachers of English, Charlotte, NC, April 10–12.

Fry, E. 1997. E-mail correspondence, "CATENet: Open Letter to the President" posted by Jim Burke/CATENet, June 19.

Golub, J. 1993. "The Voices We Hear." *English Leadership Quarterly* 15 (2): 2–5.

Goodman, K. 1997. E-mail correspondence, "CATENet: Goodman on Standards" posted by Jim Burke/CATENet, February 3.

Goodman, Y. 1978. "Kid Watching: An Alternative to Testing." *National Elementary Principals Journal* 57: 41–45.

Goodrich, H. December 1996/January 1997. "Understanding Rubrics." *Educational Leadership* 54 (4): 14–17.

Graves, D., and B. Sunstein. 1992. *Portfolio Portraits.* Portsmouth, NH: Heinemann.

Gronlund, N. 1985. *Measurement and Evaluation in Teaching.* 5th ed. New York: Macmillan.

"Gunning for Better Grades." 1997 (January 22). *Butler Eagle* 127 (276): 11.

Gwizdala, C. 1997. Reaching Out to Parents. Paper presented at annual meeting of National Council of Teachers of English, Charlotte, NC, April 10–12.

Hall, B. W. 1985. "Survey of the Technical Characteristics of Published Educational Achievement Tests." *Educational Measurement: Issues and Practice* 4 (Spring): 6–14.

Hammill, D., L. Brown, and B. R. Bryant. 1989. *A Consumer's Guide to Tests in Print.* Austin, TX: Pro-Ed.

Harp, B., ed. 1994. *Assessment and Evaluation in Student-Centered Classrooms.* 2nd ed. Norwood, MA: Christopher-Gordon.

Hayes-Parvin, K. 1997. Building Community with Parents, Students, and Teachers. Paper presented at annual meeting of National Council of Teachers of English, Charlotte, NC, April 10–12.

Irmscher, W. 1984. *Teaching Expository Writing.* New York: Holt, Rinehart and Winston.

Jago, C. 1997. "With Standards and Cleats for All" *The Outlook* February 28, D1.

Kelly-Garris, K. 1993. In *UN-Covering the Curriculum*, edited by K. and J. Strickland. Portsmouth, NH: Boynton/Cook.

Kerr, C. 1991. "Is Education Really All That Guilty?" *Education Week* (February 27): 30.

Kessler, R. 1996. "I Before E, Except After Me." Hempfield Area High School, PA.

King-Shaver, B. 1992. "Process-Based Literature/Writing Examinations." *English Leadership Quarterly* 14 (1): 6–7.

———. 1996. Freshman Project Handout. South Brunswick High School, Monmouth, NJ.

Kirst, M. W., and C. Mazzeo. 1996. "The Rise, Fall, and Rise of State Assessment in California: 1993–1996." *Phi Delta Kappan* 78 (4): 319–324.

Kohn, A. 1993. *Punished by Rewards: The Trouble with Gold Stars, Incentive Plans, As, Praise, and Other Bribes.* Boston, MA: Houghton Mifflin.

Krumboltz, J., and C. Yehn. 1996. "Competitive Grading Sabotages Good Teaching." *Phi Delta Kappan* 78 (4): 324–326.

Kusic, M. 1996. "Evaluations." Hempfield Area High School, PA.

Leo, J. 1996. "Shakespeare vs. Spiderman." *U.S. News and World Report* 120 (April 1): 61.

Macrorie, K. 1988. *The I-Search Paper*. Portsmouth, NH: Boynton/Cook.

Mager, R. 1973. *Measuring Instructional Intent*. Belmont, CA: Fearon-Pittman.

Mahoney, J. 1997. E-mail correspondence, January 24.

Mandrell, L. 1997. "Zen and the Art of Grade Motivation." *English Journal* 86 (1): 28–31.

Meloy, H. 1997. Essay. Derry Area High School, PA.

Micheels, W., and M. R. Karnes. 1950. *Measuring Educational Achievement*. New York: McGraw-Hill.

Milton, O., H. Pollio, and J. Eison. 1986. *Making Sense of College Grades*. San Francisco, CA: Jossey-Bass.

Mondock, S. L. 1997. "Portfolios—The Story Behind the Story." *English Journal* 86 (1): 59–64.

A Nation at Risk: The Imperatives for Educational Reform. 1983. Washington, DC: U.S. Department of Education.

NCTE/IRA Joint Task Force on Assessment. 1996. "Standards for the Assessment of Reading and Writing." September 26. http://www.ncte.org/idea/assess/asses-in.html.

Neal, M. 1997. Personal correspondence. January 7.

———. 1998. "The Politics and Perils of Portfolio Grading." In *The Theory and Practice of Grading Writing: Problems and Possibilities*, edited by F. Zak and C. Weaver. Albany, NY: SUNY Press.

O'Donnell, C. 1994. "Dependence and Grade Inflation—A Vicious Cycle." *English Leadership Quarterly* 16 (1): 8–9.

Oliver, E. 1996. "All You Ever Wanted to Know About Assessing English but Were Afraid to Ask." E-mail correspondence, December 30.

Patterson, K. 1997. Journal Entry (#4): "On Calkins; Poetry." March 12.

Phillips, R. 1968. *Evaluation in Education*. Columbus, OH: Charles Merrill.

Popham, W. J. 1988. "Texas Educational Assessment of Minimum Skills—Reading Skills Test." *Educational Evaluation*. 2nd ed. Englewood Cliffs, NJ: Prentice Hall.

Rider, J. 1996. Grappling with Gradelessness. Unpublished manuscript, Mesa State College.

Romano, T. 1987. *Clearing the Way: Working with Teenage Writers*. Portsmouth, NH: Boynton/Cook.

Romberg, T. A. 1993. "NCTM's Standards: A Rallying Flag for Mathematics Teachers." *Educational Leadership* 50 (2): 36–41.

Rose, M. 1995. *Possible Lives: The Promise of Public Education in America*. New York: Penguin.

Rosenblatt, L. M. 1978. *The Reader, the Text, and the Poem: The Transactional Theory of the Literary Work*. Carbondale: Southern Illinois University.

St. Michel, T. 1993. "Macbeth and Sense of Self." *English Leadership Quarterly* 15 (2): 11–13.

———. 1997. Personal correspondence, January 5.

Shaw, E. 1997. "Is This What Life's About?" *Newsweek* (May 5): 22.

Shorr, T. 1996. Personal interview. Karns City Area High School, PA, October 15.

Silberman, C. 1970. *Crisis in the Classroom: The Remaking of American Education*. New York: Random House.

Simmons, K. 1997. Personal correspondence, January 3.

Smith, F. 1988. *Joining the Literacy Club*. Portsmouth, NH: Heinemann.

Sommers, J. 1991. "Bringing Practice in Line with Theory: Using Portfolio Grading in the Composition Classroom." In *Portfolios: Process and Product*, edited by P. Belanoff and M. Dickson. Portsmouth, NH: Boynton/Cook.

Spudy, B. 1996. "Dear Reader Essay." Hempfield Area High School, PA.

Standards for the English Language Arts. 1996. Urbana, IL: National Council of Teachers of English; Newark, DE: International Reading Association.

Strickland, D. 1996. American Studies Final Project. Penfield High School, Penfield, NY.

Strickland, K. 1995. *Literacy, Not Labels*. Portsmouth, NH: Boynton/Cook.

Strickland, K., and J. Strickland. 1993. *UN-Covering the Curriculum*. Portsmouth, NH: Boynton/Cook.

———. 1996. "I Do Whole Language on Fridays." *English Journal* 85 (2): 17–25.

———. 1997. "Demystifying Grading." In *Grading in the Post-Process Classroom*, edited by L. Allison, L. Bryant, and M. Hourigan. Portsmouth, NH: Boynton/Cook.

Tattersall, K. 1996. "Why Are So Many of Us Suspicious of Success?" *The Times*, 16 August, 28.

Tierney, R., M. Carter, and L. Desai. 1991. *Portfolio Assessment in the Reading-Writing Classroom*. Norwood, MA: Christopher-Gordon.

Tsujimoto, J. I. 1991. "Leadership as Shared Vision." *English Leadership Quarterly* 13 (4): 13–14.

Wansor, T. 1996. Personal correspondence, December 31.

Weaver, C. 1994. *Reading Process and Practice: From Socio-Psycholinguistics to Whole Language*. 2nd ed. Portsmouth, NH: Heinemann.

White, E. M. 1985. *Teaching and Assessing Writing*. San Francisco, CA: Jossey-Bass.

Wiggins, G. 1989a. "Teaching to the (Authentic) Test."

Educational Leadership 46 (7): 41–47.

———. 1989b. "A True Test: Toward More Authentic and Equitable Assessment." *Phi Delta Kappan* 70 (8): 703–713.

———. 1993. "Assessment: Authenticity, Context, and Validity." *Phi Delta Kappan* 75 (3): 200–214.

Wilcox, B. 1996. Smart Portfolios for Professional Development. Paper presented at annual meeting of Western Pennsylvania Council of Teachers of English, Duquesne University, PA, June 27–29.

Wonsettler, G. 1997. Personal correspondence, May 26.

Zorn, J. 1997. "The NCTE/IRA Standards: A Surrender." *English Journal* 86 (1): 83–85.

Index